Ecclesiastes:

A Participatory Study Guide

Russell L. Meek

Energion Publications
Gonzalez, FL
2013

ISBN10: 1-938434-66-8
ISBN13: 978-1-938434-66-2
Library of Congress Control Number: 2013955707

Energion Publications
P. O. Box 841
Gonzalez, FL 32560

energionpubs.com
pubs@energion.com

Praise for *Ecclesiastes: A Participatory Study Guide*

Russ Meek is one of the brightest young minds in the church today and his *Ecclesiastes: A Participatory Study Guide* is a gift to the church. In this book, Meek packages his scholarly research on Ecclesiastes in a way that is accessible to Christians who lack formal theological training. *Ecclesiastes: A Participatory Study Guide* is guaranteed to be a blessing to church members who utilize it and to the church at large.

Jason K. Allen
President, Midwestern Baptist Theological Seminary

The book of Ecclesiastes has been a passion of mine for many years. I have always been saddened by the fact that the book is often ignored in churches. The primary reason for the lack of attention is that most believers simply do not understand the book and view it as negative. Yet, there is perhaps no other book that speaks so powerfully to the modern American as does Ecclesiastes. I discovered this to be true when Russell Meek walked into my office one day and asked that I lead him through a study on Ecclesiastes. Studying the book transformed his life and renewed his faith. Russell has always been fervent about passing on the help he received from the book to others. To this end, Russell Meek has provided this much needed resource for the church in *Ecclesiastes: A Participatory Guide*. The book is written in a down to earth style that is easy and enjoyable to read. At the same time, Russell broaches the difficult questions and matters of interpretation in straightforward way. The result is a fun, thoroughly informative study that cannot fail to impact those who use it to work through the book of Ecclesiastes. We have all struggled at one time or another to understand how a good God can be at work in a world where things are not as they are supposed to be. When you are ready to figure out how to respond, open the book of Ecclesiastes and pick up Russell Meek's guide. They will help restore your hope and faith.

N. Blake Hearson
Associate Professor of OT and Hebrew
Midwestern Baptist Theological Seminary

While the academic study of Ecclesiastes has grown substantively in recent years, the book remains a hidden gem for many in the church. And tragically, fewer books could be more relevant to our postmodern, post-Christian society, which is groping for meaning in a fallen world. With the precision of an expert and the sensibility of a pastor, Russell Meek offers the church an in-depth and personal tour through one of Scripture's least explored books. Russ has long been my personal Ecclesiastes tour guide, and I am now thankful others have the chance to learn from him as well.

William R. Osborne
Assistant Professor of Biblical and Theological Studies
College of the Ozarks

Russell Meek gives an insightfully fresh perspective on the hidden treasures of Ecclesiastes by showing why the book has often been misjudged as "negative," when instead, it should be seen as an encouragement. Through this wonderful six-week journey, the reader will see powerfully expressed that life should not be seen as "vanity," but rather as a brief and transient vapor that should be thoroughly enjoyed!

D. Kevin Brown
Pastor, Mt. Pleasant Baptist Church in Wilkesboro, NC
Author of *Rite of Passage for the Home and Church*

This book is a careful, scholarly, and yet devotional reading of one of the most thought-provoking books of the Bible. It is an excellent companion to the Book of Ecclesiastes.

Allan R. Bevere
Pastor, First United Methodist Church, Akron, Ohio
Professional Fellow in Theology
Ashland Theological Seminary, Ashland, Ohio

For Brittany, who has listened to my ramblings about Ecclesiastes since she met me, and who convinces me more every day that "he who finds a wife finds a good thing, and has obtained favor from Yahweh" (Prov 18:22).

THE PARTICIPATORY STUDY SERIES

The Participatory Study Series from Energion Publications is designed to invite Bible students to become a part of the community of faith that produced the texts we now have as Scripture by studying them empathetically and with an aim to learn and grow spiritually.

The section "Using this Book" and the appendices are designed for the series and adapted to the particular study guide. Each author is free to emphasize different resources in the study, and individual students, group leaders, and teachers are encouraged to enhance their study through the use of additional resources.

It is our prayer at Energion Publications that each study guide will lead you deeper into Scripture and more importantly closer to the One who inspired it.

— Henry Neufeld, General Editor

Table of Contents

Using this Book

This study guide consists of three sections:

1. Introductory information
2. Six lessons
3. Appendix

We recommend that you first read Appendix A: Participatory Bible Study to learn the approach to Bible study used in this series. This guide is built around that approach and it will provide a helpful starting point for understanding how the guide approaches the text.

You should also have some kind of guideline for how you will approach your study. This guide is going to suggest a process of study, which I'll repeat briefly here:

1. Preparation, including materials, prayer, and opening your mind
2. Overview
3. Background
4. The inner cycle (or central loop): Meditate, Question, Research, Compare
5. Sharing

This is a study process that says very little about what you might do at each step of the process. It is, however, built on the principles of *lectio divina*, or "holy reading." Let's summarize those principles before we look at the steps to see how they will help you apply these same principles to your study.

Holy Reading: A Model for Bible Study

Lectio divina, which means holy reading, is an ancient practice of studying Scripture. There are many ways to practice *lectio divina*, as evidenced by the many ways it has been practiced since Origen first described it around 220 A.D. The great monastic traditions of the church further developed it into distinct phases and practices. The basic principle is that reading and studying the Bible should be remarkably different than reading the morning paper or studying Shakespeare. The Bible is a sacred text; it is a Living Word. It should not, therefore, be studied as if it were a collection of dead pages from history.

When the two men were walking down the Road to Emmaus, they met the risen Christ but did not recognize him (Luke 24). As they were walking down the road, Jesus interpreted the biblical story for them. Only later, as they were breaking bread, did they realize that Christ was with them the entire time.

Lectio Divina is a practice that, through the power of the Holy Spirit, invites the risen Christ to interpret Scripture to us anew. It is a prayerful reading of Scripture that expects God to speak once again through this holy Word. Prayer should influence the way you study the Bible, and studying the Bible should influence the way you pray. In *lectio divina*, it is impossible to tell when you are studying and when you are praying, as there is no difference.

This practice is usually applied on small passages of Scripture for an extended period of time. However, in this study *lectio divina* is used as a strategy to study an entire book of the Bible. This is somewhat challenging because the text is so large, but the prayerful approach is still crucial to Christian study of Scripture. In these lessons, the ancient practice of *lectio* is blended with modern study methods that take into account the historical, cultural, and literary contexts.

The historical methods are important to us because they help connect us to people of a different time and place who experienced the same God that we do, learned from the same texts, and were led by the same Spirit. In this context we do not study history for its own sake; we study history so that we might meet those who wrote the texts and those who have studied the passages before us.

The lessons in this guide are designed around the four movements of *lectio divina* established by Guigo II, a twelfth-century Carthusian monk, in a book called *The Monk's Ladder*. He organized the practice around four rungs that help us draw closer to God through reading the Bible.

Reading (*lectio*): The first rung of the ladder is reading. Believe it or not this is the step most often skipped or diminished. It is important to complete the Bible reading for each lesson in order to get the most out of it. Ideally the biblical book should be read several times so that you can become familiar with its language and themes. This book is a guide to help you study the biblical text. It is a supplement to the text itself, and the text of Scripture should be the primary focus in your study. The steps of the participatory study method emphasize different ways of reading to help the text become part of you as you study.

Meditating (*meditatio*): The next step is to meditate prayerfully on the text. Dig deep into it. Study the words. Break it down into pieces. In this study this is where the most of the background information is located. Look up words to find their meaning. Notice if there are any words or actions that the Holy Spirit may be leading you to examine further.

Praying (*oratio*): Third, we learn to pray the text. Use what you have learned from the Scripture to formulate a prayer. It may be helpful to write it down. At the beginning of each lesson is a prayer that expounds on the themes from the text. Feel free to add your own prayers. This is where the text really becomes alive to us.

In the method used for this study guide, prayer is not seen as simply one part of the study; prayer permeates your study. You start with prayer and listening so that you will hear what God has to say through the text. Then you end by turning what you have heard from God back into prayer. The prayer never ceases!

Contemplating (*contemplatio*): The last step is the most difficult and rewarding. You have read the text, studied the text, and prayed the text. Now it is time to *be* the text. Let it seep into your being. Be still and listen. Make sure you leave some time after prayer for silence and reflection. It is said that Dan Rather once interviewed Mother Theresa about her prayer life. Rather asked her, "What do you say to God when you pray?" Her answer was simple: "I don't say anything. I just listen." After that he asked, "Well, what does Jesus say to you?" And Mother Theresa answered, "Oh, he doesn't say anything, either. He just listens." Listening is what is important. You may not always feel anything, but God is there. Another facet of contemplation is to learn to do the text. We cannot be just hearers of the word; we must also be doers of the word. Let the Scripture change the way you live your life.

Applying the Principles in Participatory Study

Preparation

As you begin the study, preparation will involve getting the materials you want to use, then prayer to begin each session of study. Part of this introductory time will be making decisions about the time and resources you can devote to this study. This is also your time of prayer. Before you begin to read, pray. Then listen. You come to the text because God calls you to it.

Overview

Read Ecclesiastes through at least once, but preferably three times. Don't feel bad about how many times you read. Choose a number that seems reasonable to you. This is part of *lectio,* but only part. You will learn to read in other ways in different phases of your study. Once you have read Ecclesiastes through your chosen number of times, read one or two of the following:

The entry on Ecclesiastes in a Bible handbook;

The entry on Ecclesiastes in a Bible dictionary;

The introductory note on Ecclesiastes in your study Bible, if you're using one;

The introductory section of a good commentary on Ecclesiastes (see Appendix B for resource details).

Here is where we introduce historical elements into your study. Don't imagine that God cannot talk to you through this text because you are so far separated from the people who wrote it. They were people like you who had hopes, dreams, gifts, and failings. Study the background to help you connect to them. Christianity is a community that extends not only in space right now but in time.

The Central Loop

For this overview, your central loop, as I call it, is your whole study of the book. Keep in mind that no element of your study is something you do just once and then forget about it. Prayer is continuous. There are multiple ways of reading, questioning, studying, and sharing.

For this study, I have divided Ecclesiastes into six thematic lessons.

1. Introduction to Ecclesiastes
2. The Meaning of *Hebel*

3. The Brevity of Life and Inescapability of Death
4. The Problem of Injustice
5. The Impetus to Enjoy
6. The Importance of Obedience

The central loop is most closely related to *meditatio*, but the implementation of *meditatio* extends into the next section where you question the text in a directed way. Don't concentrate on the boundaries between one activity and the next. They are all related!

Within each unit there will be an opportunity to think of new questions one might ask for further study. Generating new questions helps keep us from getting stale. Not only do I not have all the answers; I don't even have all the questions! Think of a question primarily as a way to prepare your mind to hear the text. When we listen or read, we often hear what we expect to hear. If I'm listening to the radio for weather, I may miss a major discussion of politics. You can miss what God is saying to you through a biblical author because you are looking for something else. Questioning is an important part of *meditatio*, but it also relates closely to *oratio*—take your questions to God in prayer.

Finally, find something to share. Remember that sharing can be in the form of a question. For example, one might ask others how they understand a particular word, such as "incarnation," "poverty," or "atonement." Take notes on their answers, and bring that information back to your study. Then ask yourself what your neighbors will hear when you make particular statements, such as "I must be bold for Jesus!" or "Jesus is the only way to receive atonement." Do those statements mean something to them? Do they mean the same thing to them as they do to you?

This is part of *contemplatio* as you try to be and to do the text. We often think of sharing primarily as telling someone things that we have learned. But if what you learned is that God loves prisoners, for example, you might find that the best way of sharing that lesson is to become active in prison ministry. Sharing demonstrates that you don't believe the text is your private possession. It is God's gift to the Christian community.

Resources

The following resources are referenced regularly in the text. In a small group it is a good idea to have different members of the group bring different reference works. For individual study, use a selection:

Study Bibles

There are many study Bibles available. Some take a more scholarly approach, while others are devotional. In selecting a study Bible, it is best to begin by selecting a specific translation and then find a study Bible based upon that text. The New International Version (NIV) is very popular and there are a large number of study Bibles related to it. While the NIV emerged from evangelical Protestantism, most mainline Protestant churches use the New Revised Standard Version. Many evangelical churches, especially in the Reformed tradition, use the English Standard Version (ESV). There is an excellent study Bible for this version, titled simply *The ESV Study Bible*. For easier reading along with an evangelical approach, the *NLT Study Bible* is an excellent choice as well. If your choice is the NRSV then the leading options are: *The New Oxford Annotated Bible, New Interpreter's Study Bible, The Harper-Collins Study Bible*, and *The Access Bible*. Again, these are not the only translations or study Bibles available for consultation, especially since the ones mentioned are based on the New Revised Standard Version.

A note on study Bibles in general—one should be careful to separate the text from the commentary. It is easy to confuse them since they are placed together. It is, of course, always good to look at resources from a variety of perspectives, and thus resources beyond one's study Bible should be consulted. Look at materials you are likely to disagree with in order to stimulate your thinking. (See

Appendix B for information on these resources. The Participatory Bible Study web site, http://www.deepbiblestudy.com, is regularly updated with ideas about materials.)

Concordances

You may decide to consult either English language concordances, or those that include material on the original languages. If you get a concordance, find one that matches the Bible version you use. Besides print versions there are a number of free online sites that are helpful including Bible Gateway (multiple translations) and the Oremus Bible Browser.

Bible Dictionaries

The information in a good Bible dictionary overlaps what is found in many study Bibles and Bible handbooks, but Bible dictionaries can be very useful for general study of topics being considered. It is important that to purchase an up-to-date Bible dictionary. See the resource list for suggestions.

Bible Handbooks

The information found in a Bible handbook will be similar to what is found in many study Bibles, only it will lack the biblical text.

Bible Commentaries

These resources offer more detailed exegetical explanations and interpretation of the actual text. They range from one-volume to multiple volumes. For the Old Testament, I would recommend purchase of volumes in the NIV Application Commentary series. In purchasing commentaries, it is best to stay away from sets such as Matthew Henry or Jameson, Fausset, and Brown. These were written several centuries ago and lack the kinds of historical and linguistic information you will need for deeper study. They have devotional value, but they can be found online.

When it comes to comparing passages you will find your study Bible, concordance, and any Bible with reference notes to be very useful. Remember, however, that even the cross-references are just someone's opinion of how one passage is related to another. You don't have to agree. Look at the passages yourself and ask not just whether they are related, but how they are related.

Remember to keep an open mind and a receptive heart while studying the Bible. Study prayerfully. Meditate on what you read. Try to place yourself in the audience of people who might have first heard this book.

The following pamphlets in the Participatory Study Series from Energion Publications, which can be found online at http://www.participatorystudyseries.com, may also be helpful in your study:

- ✓ What's in a Version?
- ✓ What is Biblical Criticism?
- ✓ I Want to Pray
- ✓ The Authority of the Bible
- ✓ What is the Word of God?

Henry Neufeld, General Editor[1]

1 Each author contributes modifications to this section in order to place the focus on the topic of their particular volume. I would particularly like to thank Dr. Geoffrey Lentz, my co-author for the book *Learning and Living Scripture*, who contributed heavily to the portions on *lectio divina*.

Introduction

The book of Ecclesiastes began to call my name some years ago, during a time of deep pain and searching for God. I turned to the book because I thought that in it I would find a kindred spirit, a voice that would concur with my own. I longed for some biblical figure who would agree with me that this life is meaningless. I read Ecclesiastes because I thought the book's author had lived through very difficult times, had doubted God, had deemed all of life vanity, and yet somehow had managed to hang on to his faith in God. So, in a last attempt to keep hold of my childhood faith, I asked a professor at seminary to construct an independent study—a class with only the two of us—so that I could study the book in an academic setting and earn credit toward my degree. During that year of study I learned many things about the book of Ecclesiastes, things that have drastically changed my life and showed me that Ecclesiastes is even more important and applicable to the modern-day follower of Christ than I first thought.

Many people read the book of Ecclesiastes the same way I did at first, thinking that the author was more than likely clinically depressed, teetering on the precipice of despair. But, I contend that this is not the case at all. The author of Ecclesiastes was no pessimist who walked around talking about how "meaningless" or "vain" life is. No, the author was a man of great faith who looked at the world around him and realized that something was not quite right. You, me, all of us have done the very same thing. For me, the first time I thought, "something is wrong here" was when my grandmother died when I was ten or eleven years old. Here was a woman who loved the Lord to her dying day, singing "Amazing Grace" while her hair fell out in clumps because of the chemotherapy that wreaked as much havoc as the cancer inside of her. How in the world does a good God let that happen to a woman who loves Him so dearly? Something was wrong.

The author of Ecclesiastes noticed similar things: "the race is not to the swift, nor the battle to the strong, nor bread to the wise, nor riches to the intelligent, nor favor to those with knowledge, but time and chance happen to them all" (Eccl 9:11). Not only does "time and chance" happen to everyone, but justice and righteousness get tangled up with injustice and unrighteousness (Eccl 3:16). Where we expect one, we find the other. Most defeating of all, though, is that death wraps its arms around all of us: "For what happens to the children of man and what happens to the beast is the same; as one dies, so dies the other. They all have the same breath, and man has no advantage over the beasts . . ." (Eccl 3:19). Something is wrong.

There are injustices in this world. There will be suffering until that day that Jesus returns in all of his glory to take believers to the place where there will be no tears and no death. This is the place where the author of Ecclesiastes longed to go. For now, we are left in the in-between time, a time that is full of death, full of tears, full of longing for intimacy with God. It is in this world that Ecclesiastes must be heard in full. The book's message is one that offers hope to people who struggle with life's injustices. It doesn't sweep difficult situations under the rug, so to speak. The author of Ecclesiastes takes a long, hard look at life in this world and states honestly that things haven't gone quite the way they were supposed to. The book's message is therefore this:

- ✓ Life is full of death and injustice; bad stuff happens to good people and good stuff happens to bad people.
- ✓ People have no real power to change anything: we are all at the mercy of God in heaven.
- ✓ Therefore, we must enjoy the temporary gifts that God gives: food, work, and a spouse.
- ✓ However, we must be careful to stay within the boundaries God has set: "fear God and keep his commandments, for

> this is the whole duty of man. For God will bring every deed into judgment, with every secret thing, whether good or evil" (Ecc 12:13–14).

This study guide will examine Ecclesiastes in order to show how it develops this message of enjoyment and rest in God. Lesson one will lay the foundation necessary to examine the book in its original context by looking at the authorship of Ecclesiastes, its historical setting, and its literary setting. Lesson two will look at the meaning of the book's key word, *hebel* (pronounced "hevel"), which has traditionally been translated into English with words such as "vanity" and "meaningless." Lesson three will examine how Ecclesiastes deals with the brevity of life and the injustice of death. Lesson four looks at the breakdown between actions and consequences, the fact that good things happen to bad people and bad things happen to good people. Lesson five looks at Ecclesiastes's answer to the problems it has raised: enjoy the gifts of God. Finally, lesson six reminds us that God is sovereign and that we must trust him and enjoy his gifts within the boundaries that he has established. Each chapter will end with several discussion questions designed to facilitate further exploration of the book in a small group or Sunday School setting.

The book of Ecclesiastes has a very important message for believers today. I invite you to open your heart and mind as we explore its meaning and importance for your life.

Lesson One

Objective: Upon completion of this lesson, you will have a basic understanding of the historical context, literary context, and authorship of the book of Ecclesiastes. This knowledge will aid in understanding and applying the book as a whole by allowing you to place it within its proper context, both historically and literarily.

Opening Prayer: Dear God, thank you for your goodness and grace. Please open my heart and mind to understand your Word and to apply it to my life. I give thanks to you for the opportunity to study your Word and pray that I will be able to use what I learn here to glorify you in the rest of my life. May your kingdom come and your will be done in my life as it is in heaven. In Jesus's name, Amen.

Weekly Reading: Since this is the first week of your study of Ecclesiastes, I encourage you to read the entire book in one sitting each day this week. While this may seem overwhelming at first (an entire book of the Bible!), Ecclesiastes is actually a rather short book. Reading all twelve chapters should take around 20–30 minutes, the same amount of time it would take to watch an episode of your favorite sitcom. The reason I am asking you to read the entire book every day this week is that doing so will give you a good grasp of the author's thought process. If you already have a good grasp of what the book actually says, then you will learn much more from your time with this study guide.

Lesson Outline:

1. Who wrote Ecclesiastes?
2. When was Ecclesiastes written?
3. What type of literature is Ecclesiastes and why does it matter?

Who Wrote Ecclesiastes?

The question of the authorship of Ecclesiastes has been debated for nearly as long as the book has been around. I am afraid that I will not be able to settle a question that has stumped so many other interpreters, but I can give you a pretty good understanding of who probably wrote the book.

Who is this "Preacher"?

The first issue that we need to look at is the word that the speaker in the book uses to refer to himself: Qoheleth. Qoheleth is a Hebrew term that is translated with different English words depending on which translation you read. For example, the NIV and HCSB (Holman Christian Standard Bible) call Qoheleth "the Teacher." Most other modern translations opt for a term that is familiar to all of us: "the Preacher."

The reason these translations call our speaker "the Teacher" or "the Preacher" is that the Hebrew word "Qoheleth" means something like "one who assembles" or "one who gathers" or even "one who convenes." These phrases most certainly bring to mind preachers and teachers. After all, preachers and teachers often gather crowds around them to tell stories and teach about God. Essentially, this is what the speaker in the book of Ecclesiastes is doing: teaching his audience (and now us) about God and how to live a godly life in a broken world. Thus, many translations simply call him "the Preacher." In this book we will call him by his Hebrew name, as if he were an old friend: Qoheleth.

Who is Qoheleth? A Brief History of Interpretation

Early Interpreters

Solomon has historically been identified as Qoheleth, and thus the author of Ecclesiastes. Solomon's identification as the author of Ecclesiastes is based on several passages within the book, such as Ecclesiastes 1:1, 12, and the description of his riches and wealth in Ecclesiastes 2. An early Jewish commentary on Ecclesiastes, *Targum Qoheleth*, identifies Solomon as the author of Ecclesiastes and relates a brief story to explain how he came to write the book:

> When King Solomon of Israel was sitting on his royal throne, his heart became very proud because of his wealth, and he transgressed the decree of the Memra of the Lord; he gathered many horses, chariots, and cavalry; he collected much silver and gold; he married foreign peoples. Immediately the anger of the Lord grew strong against him. Therefore, He sent Ashmedai king of the demons, against him who drove him from his royal throne and took his signet ring from his hand so that he would wander and go into exile in the world to chastise him. He went about in all the districts and towns of the Land of Israel. He wept, pleaded, and said, "I am Qoheleth, who was previously named Solomon. I was king over Israel in Jerusalem."[1]

Readers today may be tempted to scoff at such fanciful stories. An evil demon? Really? However, the ancient interpreters were simply trying to make sense of how the book came to be written. Since the book itself states "I *was* king over Israel in Jerusalem" (Eccl 1:12, emphasis mine), Jewish interpreters provide an explanation for a time when Solomon was not king over Israel in Jerusalem, and thus preserve the truthfulness of the Bible.

Later Christian interpreters, such as Origen, Gregory of Nyssa, Augustine, John Chrysostom, and Gregory Thaumaturgos followed the Jewish tradition of identifying Qoheleth with Solomon.[2]

Despite the widespread agreement regarding Solomonic authorship of many early interpreters of the book, a few important scholars argued that Solomon did not write Ecclesiastes. For example, Didymus the Blind states that "[a]ctually the Spirit is the

1 *The Targum of Qoheleth* (ed. and trans. Peter S. Knobel; The Aramaic Bible 15; Edinburgh: T & T Clark, 1991), 22.

2 Eric Christianson, *Ecclesiastes through the Centuries* (Blackwell Bible Commentaries; Malden, MA: Blackwell, 2007), 92–93.

author of the divinely inspired Scriptures . . . Either the real author is Solomon, or some [other] wise men have written it. Maybe we should opt for the latter so that nobody may say that the speaker talks about himself."[1] The Babylonian Talmud was likewise unconvinced that Solomon was Qoheleth, stating that "Hezekiah and his colleagues wrote . . . Isaiah, Proverbs, the Song of Songs and Ecclesiastes" (*b. Baba Bathra* 15a). The Talmud's view is repeated by several other rabbinic commentators, such as Isaac ibn Ghiyath (1038–1089), David Kimchi (1160–1235), and Samuel ibn Tibbon (1150-1230.[2] Therefore, while many of the early Jewish and Christian writers agreed that Qoheleth was none other than Solomon, there were doubts even at this early stage.

Interpretation in the Reformation and Beyond: The Fall of Solomon as Author

The Reformation was a period of great change in the Christian church. Reformers such as Martin Luther, John Calvin, and Ulrich Zwingli cried out for a return to the Bible and made translations available in the languages of the common people. These bold men changed the course of Christian history, but what does that have to do with the authorship of Ecclesiastes?

Martin Luther was perhaps the most important Christian interpreter to suggest that Solomon may not have written Ecclesiastes. In his commentary on Ecclesiastes Luther argues that Ecclesiastes was Solomonic *in origin*, but was composed by a later group of "disciples."[3] However, in his famous *Table Talk*, Luther goes even further by asserting that "he [Solomon] himself did not write the

1 Didymus the Blind, *Commentary on Ecclesiastes* 7.9, in *Proverbs, Ecclesiastes, and Song of Solomon* (Ancient Christian Commentary on Scripture IX; ed. J. Robert Wright; Downers Grove, IL: InterVarsity, 2005), 192.

2 Christianson, *Ecclesiastes through the Centuries*, 96.

3 Martin Luther, *An Exposition of Salomons Booke Called Ecclesiastes or the Preacher* (London: John Daye, 1573), 9. See Craig Bartholomew, *Ecclesiastes* (Baker Commentary on the Old Testament Wisdom and Psalms; Grand Rapids, MI: Baker Academic, 2009), 44.

book, but it was composed at the time of the Maccabees, by Sirach."[1] With this statement, Luther opened the door for the critical scholarship that was to follow a few centuries later.[2]

Most modern scholars argue that Solomon was not the author of Ecclesiastes based on the style of the Hebrew that was used to compose the book, as well as a few words that entered the Hebrew vocabulary long after Solomon died. Other features that scholars use to argue against Solomonic authorship are passages that seem to indicate influence from Greek philosophy and historical situations that are distant in time from Solomon. However, we will see below that these arguments are far from conclusive and there are many good reasons to hold to Solomonic authorship.

Arguments for and against Solomon as the Author of Ecclesiastes

It is clear that throughout history the authorship of Ecclesiastes has been in question. The question for us, though, is why have people doubted that he wrote the book? Additionally, we must ask whether there is any evidence that would tell us who did in fact

---

1 Martin Luther, *Luthers Werke*, 1:207, cited by Bartholomew, *Ecclesiastes*, 44. However, note Eric Christianson (*Ecclesiastes through the Centuries*, 95), who follows Theodore Preston in arguing that Luther does not in fact deny Solomonic authorship in this text (*The Hebrew Text, and a Latin Version of the Book of Solomon Called Ecclesiastes; with Original Notes, Philological and Exegetical, and a Translation of the Commentary of Mendlessohn from the Rabbinic Hebrew; Also a Newly Arranged Version of Ecclesiastes* [London: John W. Parker, 1845]), 12.

2 By "critical" scholarship, I am referring to "an approach to the study of scripture that is centrally concerned with searching for and applying neutral, i.e., scientific and nonsectarian, canons of judgment in its investigation of the biblical text" (Richard N. Soulen and R. Kendall Soulen, *Handbook of Biblical Criticism* [3d ed.; Louisville, KY: Westminster John Knox, 2001], 18). Generally speaking, critical scholarship eschews "faith-based," or confessional, interpretations of the Bible. I would like to thank William K. Bechtold, III for this reference.

write Ecclesiastes. In this section we will look at various passages within the book that may indicate who Qoheleth was.

Does Qoheleth Directly Claim to Be Solomon?

There are several passages within the book of Ecclesiastes that seem to indicate that Solomon is Qoheleth. This should come as no surprise given the fact that many people have credited him with writing the book throughout history. The first such verses come at the very beginning of the book: "The words of Qoheleth, son of David, king in Jerusalem" (Eccl 1:1) and "I, Qoheleth, was king over Israel in Jerusalem" (Eccl 1:12). If we take these verses at face value, then there are very few people who actually fit the bill. The person whose words are recorded in Ecclesiastes was a son of David and a king *over Israel* in Jerusalem, which seems to suggest that Qoheleth must have been either Solomon or Rehoboam because no other king ruled Israel from Jerusalem after them. Some scholars argue that the term "son" in this passage could refer to a descendant of David, thus opening the door for the "son of David" to be someone other than an immediate child of David. However, the eminent scholar C. L. Seow has rightly pointed out that the phrase does in fact always mean an actual immediate child in the Old Testament.[1] Therefore, we are still left with basically two options: Rehoboam and Solomon. It is highly unlikely that Rehoboam is Qoheleth because he only reigned over Israel in Jerusalem for a very short period, which leaves us with the logical conclusion that Solomon is Qoheleth.

But, let's not jump to conclusions too quickly here. What might be the problem with this interpretation of Ecclesiastes 1:1, 12? There was never a time in Solomon's life when he could say that he *was* king over Israel in Jerusalem. This very fact is what led the authors of the Talmud to concoct the story about the evil demon

1 C. L. Seow, *Ecclesiastes: A New Translation with Introduction* (Anchor Bible 18C; New York: Doubleday, 1997), 97. Cited in Daniel C. Fredericks and Daniel J. Estes, *Ecclesiastes and the Song of Songs* (Apollos Old Testament Commentary; Downers Grove, IL: Intervarsity, 2010), 31.

who ruled in Solomon's place. This may not be as insurmountable a problem as many suppose, however, because the Hebrew word translated by the English word "was" can be translated in various ways. One of the ways that Ecclesiastes 1:12 can be translated is "I have been king," which is the way that many of us talk about things we are currently doing.[1] For example, I could say that I have been teaching for a few years. This does not indicate that I no longer am teaching, but that I am currently teaching and have taught in the past. Thus, the translation "I have been king," which is just as plausible as "I was king," removes the difficulty of there never having been a time in Solomon's life when he "was" king.

A few verses later, the text reads "I have acquired great wisdom, surpassing all who were over Jerusalem before me, and my heart has had great experience of wisdom and knowledge" (Eccl 1:16). Certainly this type of boasting could only come from Solomon, for we know from 1 Kings 4:30 that "Solomon's wisdom surpassed all the wisdom of the people of the east and all the wisdom of Egypt, for he was wiser than all other men …" And 1 Kings 10:23 tells us that "Solomon exceeded all the kings of the earth in riches and wisdom." However, if we read Ecclesiastes 1:16 closely, we will see that Qoheleth states that he surpassed all those in *Jerusalem* before him. This small detail is important because the only ruler who came before Solomon in Jerusalem was his father, David. Before David captured the city of Jerusalem it was ruled by Jebusite kings, so it is possible that Qoheleth refers to these rulers to in this passage. However, Tremper Longman points out that such a comparison "would be passing strange coming from an Israelite king. After all, these were pagan, alien kings, and hostile to Israel."[2] Therefore, when we read the text closely, it casts doubt on the association of Qoheleth with Solomon. Once again there may be some other way to explain the passage. Daniel Fredericks argues that the passage "does not specify that he [Solomon] was greater in wisdom than just

1 Fredericks, *Ecclesiastes*, 77.

2 Tremper Longmann III, *Ecclesiastes* (New International Commentary on the Old Testament; Grand Rapids, MI: Eerdmans, 1998), 5.

those who were kings before him, but included any predecessor in Jerusalem, such as elders, wise men, prophets and so on . . . so his statement is not to be applied simply to David, but to others such as Adoni-zedek (Josh. 10:3)."[1] Thus, if we understand this passage to refer to any ruler in Jerusalem before Solomon came to power, then it is plausible that Solomon is indeed Qoheleth. Nevertheless, it is important to note that these passages are incredibly ambiguous and can be interpreted in multiple ways. In an effort not to go beyond what Scripture says, it is best at this point to be content with the fact that Ecclesiastes does not *directly* claim Solomonic authorship.

Solomonic Texts

So, Ecclesiastes does not directly claim to have been written by Solomon. But, Bible-believing Christians throughout history and today do believe that the book was written by Solomon. The goal in looking at these passages so closely is to read the Bible carefully in order that we may know and understand it for ourselves. So, we turn now to several passages that may indicate that Solomon is Qoheleth.

First, and perhaps most famously, Ecclesiastes 2 reads as if it could be written by none other than Solomon himself:

> I made great works. I built houses and planted vineyards for myself. I made myself gardens and parks, and planted in them all kinds of fruit trees. I made myself pools from which to water the forest of growing trees. I bought male and female slaves, and had slaves who were born in my house. I had also great possessions of herds and flocks, more than any who had been before me in Jerusalem. I also gathered for myself silver and gold and the treasure of kings and provinces. I got singers, both men and women, and many concubines, the delight of the sons of man. So I became great and surpassed all who were before me in Jerusalem. Also my wisdom remained with me. And whatever my eyes desired I did not keep from them. I kept

1 Fredericks, *Ecclesiastes*, 83.

> my heart from no pleasure, for my heart found pleasure in all my toil, and this was my reward for all my toil. (Eccl 2:4–10)

The sorts of accomplishments cited in this passage are things that only a king could do. Note that once again Qoheleth claims to have surpassed all those who were before him in Jerusalem. Further, he states that he acquired the "treasures of kings and provinces" along with much silver and gold. Who else but a king could amass this sort of wealth?

There were two primary ways that a king would amass wealth in the ancient Near East: through receiving gifts from other monarchs and through taxation, whether taken from his own subjects or from conquered lands. First Kings 10 records a good example of the type of gift-giving that was the custom in the ancient Near East:

> Now when the queen of Sheba heard of the fame of Solomon concerning the name of the LORD, she came to test him with hard questions. She came to Jerusalem with a very great retinue, with camels bearing spices and very much gold and precious stones. And when she came to Solomon, she told him all that was on her mind.... Then she gave the king 120 talents of gold, and a very great quantity of spices and precious stones. Never again came such an abundance of spices as these that the queen of Sheba gave to King Solomon. Moreover, the fleet of Hiram, which brought gold from Ophir, brought from Ophir a very great amount of almug wood and precious stones. (1 Kgs 10:1–2, 10–11)

Having heard of Solomon's fame, the Queen of Sheba visited him to "test him with hard questions" and was careful to bring along gifts that would be fitting for such a wise and wealthy king. Not only that, but the Bible also records that when she left, Solomon returned the favor of her extravagant giving by giving her anything for which she asked.

The second way that a king would secure revenue, through taxation of his people or of conquered people, is also evident in Solomon's life. We can detect his heavy taxation of the people in the narratives that recount how he built the temple and his palace and secured fantastic provisions for his own household (see 1 Kgs 4–10). The text makes the people's dissatisfaction with the tax burden explicit when Rehoboam takes over after Solomon's death. The people plead with Rehoboam to lessen their load, stating "Your father made our yoke heavy. Now therefore lighten the hard service of your father and his heavy yoke on us, and we will serve you" (1 Kgs 12:4). First Kings also recounts how Solomon conscripted laborers from conquered people to build his great projects (1 Kgs 9:15–22).

Finally, it is clear from the biblical narrative that God blessed Solomon with extravagant wealth as a result of his request for wisdom to rule God's people (1 Kgs 10:10–14). Solomon used all of this wealth, along with the laborers from Israel and other lands, to construct massive building projects throughout Jerusalem. Most famously, Solomon built the first temple for Yahweh, a task that his father David had wanted to complete (1 Kgs 6:1–38). After completing the temple, Solomon built exquisite palaces both for himself and at least one of his wives (1 Kgs 7:1–12). From the narrative in 1 Kings, then, it seems likely that Qoheleth is indeed Solomon. Who else in Israel could fit the description in Ecclesiastes 2? In the words of C. L. Seow, these verses "call to mind the activities and fabulous wealth of Solomon in 1 Kgs 3–11. Indeed it is difficult not to think of Solomon when the author concludes in 2:9 that he 'became great and surpassed' all who preceded him in Jerusalem.'"[1]

Non-Solomonic Texts?

Even though the above texts seem to close the case on Solomonic authorship, there are several other passages in Ecclesiastes that would seem to indicate an author other than Solomon. Scholars often point to these passages as evidence against Solomonic authorship because they seem to be written by a person who is either critical of the monarchy or who is powerless.[2] This perspective would be akin to the president of the United States railing against

1 Seow, *Ecclesiastes*, 150.

2 See, for example, Tremper Longman, *Ecclesiastes*, 4–6.

presidential power or lamenting the fact that he has no ability to change things that are clearly within his executive powers. Of course no one would expect such statements from the president!

Ecclesiastes 4:1–3 is the first passage that may hint that the author is writing from a different perspective than that of a king. It reads:

> Again I saw all the oppressions that are done under the sun. And behold, the tears of the oppressed, and they had no one to comfort them! On the side of their oppressors there was power, and there was no one to comfort them. And I thought the dead who are already dead more fortunate than the living who are still alive. But better than both is he who has not yet been and has not seen the evil deeds that are done under the sun.

As Tremper Longman points out, Qoheleth simply notes that there is oppression and laments its existence.[1] He does nothing to alleviate the pain of the oppressed, as would certainly be well within his power if he were indeed Israel's King Solomon.[2] Not only that, but as we saw above "he, according to the historical books, contributed heavily to it in the last days of his life (1 Kings 11)."[3] For Longman and others, the dissonance between the Solomon we see in 1 Kings and the author of this passage is a certain indicator that Qoheleth is not Solomon. However, Craig Bartholomew points out the intent of the passage, and indeed the book as a whole, is to chronicle Qoheleth's own journey through life.[4] Therefore, we should not be surprised that he simply languishes over the fact that oppression exists; it is not his aim to relieve suffering, but to suggest

---

1 Longman, *Ecclesiastes*, 133–4.

2 Robert Gordis, *Koheleth: The Man and His World* (New York: Bloch, 1962), 77.

3 Ibid., 133.

4 Bartholomew, *Ecclesiastes*, 186. Compare with Eric Christianson, *A Time to Tell: Narrative Strategies in Ecclesiastes* (Journal for the Study of the Old Testament Supplement Series 280; Sheffield: Sheffield Academic, 1998), 135.

to his hearers a way to cope in a world that is often unjust and cruel. Furthermore, Fredericks points out that "'fixing' [a problem] is not always the goal of reviewing reality. Often the review is simply to alert the morally comatose, not to offer the easy answer in a sound bite . . ."[1] Given the purpose of this passage, then, we should not be too hasty to deny its words could have originated with Solomon.

Ecclesiastes 5:8–9 is a particularly difficult text to reconcile with Solomonic authorship, for it has some very harsh words for those in power:

> If you see in a province the oppression of the poor and the violation of justice and righteousness, do not be amazed at the matter, for the high official is watched by a higher, and there are yet higher ones over them. But this is gain for a land in every way: a king committed to cultivated fields.

There are many difficulties with the translation of this verse, but the ESV represents its traditional rendering into English.[2] Here again, we find a verse that seems quite strange coming from the highest official in the land. Why would a king, who ostensibly has the power to end corruption, simply point it out and then talk about "cultivated fields"? Fredericks provides a viable interpretation of the passage when he points out that verse nine indicates that when administration occurs as it should—when the king administers justice appropriately—all benefit.[3] This is unfortunately not always the case, and so we should not be surprised when we see it because we live in a fallen world, a world in which oppression and injustice exist even at the highest levels of government. In fact, a person today would have to deliberately turn a blind eye to the atrocities committed by governments worldwide in order *not*

1 Fredericks, *Ecclesiastes*, 133.

2 For a different translation, see Tremper Longman, *Ecclesiastes*, 157. He translates the verse as: "The profit of the land is taken by all; even the king benefits from the field." For a fuller discussion on the linguistic difficulties in this passage, see Aron Pinker, "The Advantage of a Country in Ecclesiastes 5:8," *Jewish Bible Quarterly* 37 (2009): 211–22.

3 Fredericks, *Ecclesiastes*, 141.

to see oppression and injustice perpetrated by government officials. Even though it may not come as much solace to those facing such oppression, Qoheleth observes that such injustices should not occur—and indeed would not occur—in a land whose highest official cultivates his "field" properly. Even though this text reads like "protest literature against the king, not by him," it is possible to see this sentiment coming from the very person who would be in the situation to make such an assessment—the king himself.[1]

A final verse that causes some difficulty in affirming Solomonic authorship is Ecclesiastes 10:20:

> Even in your thoughts, do not curse the king, nor in your bedroom curse the rich, for a bird of the air will carry your voice, or some winged creature tell the matter.

If we were to hear these words from the mouth of a king, or perhaps our boss at work, we may find the sentiment quite unsettling. Such a statement would make us wonder what sort of boss for whom we are working. Does he have spies throughout the office who will tattle on me if I say a cross word? Perhaps a more likely candidate to deliver this message would be a coworker who has experienced the boss's wrath. The same could be said of this verse—that it seems more like a statement from a person who has been on the receiving end of the king's punishment. However, perhaps Eric Christianson is correct in his assessment of this statement—that it would be best received from a person who is intimately familiar with how kings work, namely, a king.[2]

So, Who Wrote Ecclesiastes?

This examination of textual evidence brings us back around to the beginning of our discussion with our question unanswered. Who wrote Ecclesiastes? There is considerable evidence that indicates that Solomon was in fact the book's author, or at least that the author intended for the book to be read as if Solomon wrote

---

1 Longman, *Ecclesiastes*, 6.

2 Christianson, *A Time to Tell*, 140.

it. However, there are also some passages that would cast doubt on this assessment. If Solomon wrote Ecclesiastes, then why all of the anti-royal sentiment and statements that seem to be from a person with very limited power? Despite the seemingly difficult passages, the weight of evidence stands in favor of Solomonic authorship. We showed above how the "non-Solomonic" texts could in fact have been written by Solomon, and Daniel Fredericks's theory of later scribal activity accounts for the apparently late linguistic features that some scholars point to in order to argue against Solomonic authorship.[1] It is therefore best to conclude that Solomon in fact wrote Ecclesiastes.

When was Ecclesiastes Written?

Since it is likely that Ecclesiastes underwent scribal editing at some point, it is unclear when the final form of the book was completed. Since Ecclesiastes was included in the writings of the Qumran community (the group of people associated with the Dead Sea Scrolls), we can be certain that its final form was completed no later than the second century B.C.

As we saw above, scholars disagree significantly regarding who wrote Ecclesiastes, so it is not surprising that there is also considerable debate over when the book was written. Most modern scholars posit a date of composition much later than the time of Solomon, either in the Persian Period (539 to 334 B.C.) or Hellenistic Period (331 to 31 B.C.) of Israel's history.[2] As with the evidence regarding authorship, it is difficult to be absolutely certain regarding the

1 Daniel C. Fredericks, *Qoheleth's Language: Re-Evaluating Its Nature and Date* (Ancient Near Eastern Texts and Studies 3; Lewiston, NY: Edwin Mellen, 1988), 259; cf. idem, *Ecclesiastes*, 32. See also John Sailhammer, *The Meaning of the Pentateuch: Revelation, Composition, and Interpretation* (Downers Grove, IL: InterVarsity, 2009). Sailhammer argues for Mosaic authorship of the Pentateuch coupled with later scribal editorial activity.

2 For an excellent overview of the options, see Daniel Estes, *Handbook on the Wisdom Books and Psalms: Job, Psalms, Proverbs, Ecclesiastes, Song of Songs* (Grand Rapids, MI: Baker Academic, 2005), 273–6.

book's historical context. However, there is significant evidence, along with the weight of the history of interpretation, in favor of Solomonic authorship. While it cannot be proved without a doubt, it is likely that the majority of the book was composed during the tenth century B.C., during Solomon's lifetime.

The tenth century was a period of great prosperity for the kingdom of Israel, as is clear from the account of Solomon's reign from 1 Kings. It was also a time of relative peace. The wars that David fought against the Philistines and Israel's other neighbors had secured Israel's borders, thus guaranteeing that Solomon would be free from the warfare that marked David's reign. Since Solomon was less concerned with subduing Israel's foes, he was able to devote more time and resources to her internal development. We can see this easily in Solomon's massive building projects, such as the temple and his various palaces.

This picture of prosperity is not to imply that everyone was "happy," for we saw above that Solomon made a habit of conscripting laborers to work for him and taxing their farms at home. Therefore, while the nation as a whole saw a time of great prosperity, the individuals who composed that nation were often much less prosperous. This historical context is important to understand when reading the book of Ecclesiastes because we will come across several passages that speak of oppression and death, themes one would perhaps not expect to find in a book written by such a successful king. However, Ecclesiastes views life as it actually was, which, as we know, is all too often disheartening. This brings us to a very significant question for interpreting the book of Ecclesiastes: where does it fit within the biblical canon, and more specifically, within the body of Wisdom Literature that we find in the Bible?

What Type of Literature is Ecclesiastes and Why Does It Matter?

Biblical Wisdom Literature

The book of Ecclesiastes belongs to the Wisdom Literature genre. In the Bible, this genre comprises the books of Proverbs, Job, Ecclesiastes, and Song of Songs, along with a few Psalms. Following the advice of Mark Sneed, we must be careful not to be too simplistic in defining Wisdom Literature; nevertheless, we can point to a few features that make this a distinct genre.[1] First, Wisdom Literature is marked by its "skillful combination of poetic language and form."[2] All one has to do is flip through the pages of the Bible to see that the translators have composed their translations in the form of verse, which immediately indicates to the reader that we are dealing with something other than the narrative form that makes up much of the rest of the Bible. The Wisdom Literature also addresses aspects of life that are not usually developed as fully in the rest of the Bible. For example, "Job and Ecclesiastes probe the perennial problems of evil and significance, Song of Songs develops a delightful theology of intimacy, Proverbs addresses the various ways in which wisdom is practiced in life …"[3] Another distinct feature of these books is that they are concerned with issues related to how life is lived as a human within the world. This is not to say that they are unconcerned with having a relationship with God, for to the Hebrew mind *everything* affects one's relationship with God. This is simply to say that they deal with the "earthy," day-to-day matters of living life. Each of the wisdom books in the Bible deal with daily living in a distinct way and complement each other well. Below we will look briefly at how each individual book treats life and how they all fit together.

---

1 Mark Sneed, "Is the 'Wisdom Tradition' a Tradition?" *Catholic Biblical Quarterly* 73 (2011): 50–71.

2 Estes, *Handbook on the Wisdom Books*, 9.

3 Ibid.

Proverbs

Whereas each of the other wisdom books deals with a particular facet of life, the book of Proverbs forms the foundation of biblical wisdom literature.[1] As Craig Bartholomew and Ryan O'Dowd rightly point out, "Job and Ecclesiastes deal specifically with how to live when life appears to have turned upside down . . . Proverbs represents the ABCs of wisdom when life is generally going right."[2] The book of Proverbs speaks primarily to the way that life should be lived in covenant relationship with the Lord. It tells its readers how to deal with issues such as "work, friendship, marriage, speech, money, and integrity."[3] The book of Proverbs deals with general truths, guidelines by which we should live our lives. It is highly practical and fairly easy to apply to life, but we must be careful to interpret and apply it correctly. The primary interpretative issue with Proverbs is therefore understanding that its contents are not *absolute promises* that the reader can "name and claim."[4] Instead, when life goes as it should, the wisdom of Proverbs will ring true. For this reason the book forms the foundation for wisdom in the Old Testament. A solid understanding of Proverbs enables us to live a proper life in covenant relationship with God. The other Old Testament wisdom books teach us how to respond when life does not happen as it should.

Job

The biblical story of Job is well-known by most Christians today. His story is a heart-wrenching tale of a person who follows God completely, is upright in every way, and yet suffers greatly at

---

1 Craig Bartholomew and Ryan O'Dowd, *Old Testament Wisdom Literature: A Theological Introduction* (Downers Grove, IL: InterVarsity, 2011), 74.

2 Ibid.

3 J. Scott Duvall and J. Daniel Hays, *Grasping God's Word: A Hands-On Approach to Reading, Interpreting, and Applying the Bible* (3rd ed.; Grand Rapids, MI: Zondervan, 2012), 426.

4 Ibid., 427.

the hands of the accuser. In fact, we could easily point to Job as a person who has made the wisdom of Proverbs a foundational part of his life. Not only does Job follow the wisdom of Proverbs, but his friends also rely on that type of wisdom to guide their own lives and inform their advice to Job. This leaves today's reader wondering what in the world is going on. It seems that wisdom has failed. However, readers will also likely be comforted by Job's story because there are few of us who have not experienced unexplained suffering of some sort. Indeed, even God's own Son experienced unimaginable suffering he did not deserve. Job, then, teaches believers how to respond to God when life is going awry, when they are experiencing undeserved and unexplained suffering. When Proverbs does not quite ring true, the book of Job teaches us to trust God anyway.

Song of Songs

Song of Songs, or the Song of Solomon, approaches a much happier side of life: love and marriage. For much of church history the book was interpreted allegorically as representing the relationship between Christ and the church, but this interpretation has been abandoned by most modern interpreters, who opt read the book as the intimate relationship between a man and a woman. There is significant disagreement among interpreters concerning who is speaking in the book, but it is at least clear that there are two people who love each other deeply, which the language often makes shockingly clear.[1]

Song of Songs is comprised of three main units, or movements: "the Courtship (1:2–3:5), the Wedding (3:6–5:1), and the following Life of Love (5:2–8:14)."[2] Each of these sections is filled with highly emotive language that captures the reader's attention as it describes each aspect—emotional and sexual—of a romantic relationship between a man and woman. As Duane Garrett states,

1 For an overview of interpretive options, see Estes, *Handbook on the Wisdom Books*, 396–401.

2 Ibid., 438.

> While the marriage relationship is meant to be a partnership and friendship on the deepest level, that does not mean that the sexual and emotional aspects of love between a man and a woman are themselves unworthy of the Bible's attention. Sexuality and love are fundamental to human experience; and it is altogether fitting that the Bible, as a book meant to teach the reader how to live a happy and good life, should have something to say in this area.[1]

Song of Songs deals with life turned upside-down in a positive way and teaches the reader how to respond to life in relationship with another person on the deepest level.

Ecclesiastes

Like Job, Ecclesiastes deals with life's underbelly: the frustration caused by the disconnect between one's actions and rewards and the ever present burden of impending death. In what follows, we will explore the various ways in which Ecclesiastes teaches believers today how to deal with tragedy and the tragic, and how to trust God in the midst of injustice and undeserved suffering. When combined with the foundational understanding of wisdom provided by Proverbs, these three other wisdom books will help us to remain faithful to God and enjoy his gifts in all of life's circumstances.

Conclusion

In this lesson we have explored the authorship of Ecclesiastes, the book's historical setting, and its relationship to the other three wisdom books within the Old Testament. We have concluded that the most likely candidate for the authorship of Ecclesiastes is Solomon, although the book's final form was not settled until sometime after the king's death. We also learned that the historical context is important for understanding the book's treatment of issues such as injustice. Finally, we learned that the book of Proverbs

1 Duane Garrett, *Proverbs, Ecclesiastes, Song of Songs* (New American Commentary 14; Nashville, TN: Broadman, 1993), 366.

forms the foundation for wisdom in the Old Testament, providing the basic framework for understanding how to interact with the world in everyday life.[1] The other three wisdom books supplement Proverbs by addressing specific situations in which life is turned upside-down. In the following chapters we will explore Qoheleth's message in much greater detail, beginning with a treatment of the book's key word: *hebel.*

Discussion Questions

1. In this lesson we looked at a number of factors that play a role in how we interpret the book of Ecclesiastes. Generally speaking, a book's date of writing and its authorship play a significant role in interpretation because this knowledge helps us to understand more fully the words themselves. We can be relatively certain that Solomon wrote Ecclesiastes, but we also learned that this is by no means a completely agreed upon conclusion. How does this uncertainty change the way that we read and interpret Ecclesiastes?

2. We looked at a number of different suggestions for who penned Ecclesiastes. What has led to the disagreement over the book's authorship? Does this disagreement affect your interpretation of the book's message and meaning?

3. In our discussion of the historical setting of Ecclesiastes we noted that it was likely written during a time of great prosperity in Israel. How does this compare to the socio-economic culture of the Western world today? In your reading of the book itself you have likely picked up on the fact that it has a dim view of death, which is similar to the way death is viewed in our culture. We do everything we can to avoid growing old and often fear death. Since we live in such an affluent culture, as did Solomon, in which

---

1 Duvall and Hays, *Graspoing God's Word,* 424-5.

we can have just about anything we want, where does this fear of death come from?

4. We also spent time looking at the relationship between Ecclesiastes and the rest of the Wisdom Literature in the Old Testament. How does Ecclesiastes relate to these other books? In what ways does understanding the meaning and message of the other three wisdom books impact how you understand and apply the meaning and message of Ecclesiastes?

Lesson Two

Objective: Upon completion of this lesson, you will have a basic understanding of the importance of the Hebrew word *hebel* (traditionally translated as "vanity" or "meaningless") for the meaning of Ecclesiastes. You will also have basic knowledge of the word's history of interpretation, including how various translations of the word have affected the book's interpretation throughout history. Finally, you will have a basic grasp of the concept of inner-biblical exegesis, the relationship between Genesis and Ecclesiastes, and the importance of these concepts for the meaning of Ecclesiastes.

Opening Prayer: Dear God, thank you for your goodness and grace. Please open my mind to understand your Word better as I examine the meaning of the very words you have inspired. Thank you for your Word, and please use it now to bring me into closer relationship with you. May your kingdom come and your will be done in my life as it is in heaven. In Jesus's name, Amen.

Weekly Reading: In order to understand the parts of Ecclesiastes, we must also understand the whole. As we learn more about the parts, our understanding of the whole will be modified to reflect how we understand the parts.[1] Just as last week, this week we will be looking at the book of Ecclesiastes as a whole. The key term *hebel* appears at important places throughout the book, so it is important that you have a keen understanding of the book as a whole. Please take time this week to read the book daily, which should take roughly 20–30 minutes.

---

1 See Grant R. Osborne, *The Hermeneutical Spiral: A Comprehensive Introduction to Biblical Interpretation* (Revised and Expanded ed.; Downers Grove, IL: IVP Academic, 2006), 21–33.

Lesson Outline:

1. Is everything really "vanity"? A brief history of interpretation
2. What is inner-biblical exegesis, and why does it matter?
3. Cain, Abel, and the meaning of *hebel* in Ecclesiastes

Is Everything Really "Vanity"? A Brief History of Interpretation[1]

Most modern Bibles translate the Hebrew word *hebel* with words such as "vanity" (ESV, NKJV, NAB, NASB, NRSV), "meaningless" (NIV), "futility" (HCSB), or "pointless" (CEB). By using such inherently negative words to translate *hebel*, the translators are treating the book as largely pessimistic. The result is that those who read Ecclesiastes in translation understand the book to be pessimistic or fatalistic, the ramblings of a person resigned to a life that is "meaningless." While *hebel* certainly does have a somewhat negative connotation in some contexts, its range of meaning is significantly broader than the English translations would suggest. For example, the word "bread" has a broad range of meaning. It can refer to many, many different things: banana bread, sandwich bread, or flat bread, such as pitas. However, the word "pita" has a much more limited range of meaning: it refers to a flat type of bread made from flour of some sort. But "pita" cannot be used to refer to banana bread. Similar to "bread," *hebel* has a very broad range of meaning, but it has come to be translated with a term that has a very narrow range of meaning, such as "pita." In this section I will trace the history of interpretation of *hebel* in order to show how negative translations came to dominate English renderings of Ecclesiastes as well as to highlight the many possibilities for translating the word into English.

---

1 For a fuller treatment of the issues addressed here, see Russell L. Meek, "The Meaning of *Hebel* in Qoheleth: An Intertextual Suggestion," in *The Words of the Wise are Like Goads: Engaging Qoheleth in the 21st Century* (ed. Mark Boda, Tremper Longman, and Cristian Rata; Winona Lake, IN: Eisenbrauns, 2013), 241–56.

Pre-Modern Interpretations[1]

Septuagint

The Greek translation of the Old Testament, known as the Septuagint, most likely originated because of the need for Greek speaking Jews to have the Bible in the Greek language. However, according to the *Letter of Aristeas* (which is of questionable reliability),[2] Ptolemy of Philadephus commissioned the translation of the Old Testament into Greek for his massive library. Seventy-two scribes purportedly translated the Pentateuch in seventy-two days, though this account was later expanded by Philo and others to include the entire Old Testament, as well as the detail that each translator worked in isolation and produced a translation that agreed exactly with all of the others.[3] The Septuagint is important because it is the earliest translation of the Old Testament into another language and therefore gives insight into how *hebel* was understood at the time.

The Septuagint translators used the Greek word *mataiotes* to translate each occurrence of *hebel* in Ecclesiastes. This word, like *hebel*, has a very broad range of meaning in Greek that includes terms such as "vanity," "transitory," "breath," and "emptiness." The word carries a negative connotation in some instances, but it is clear from the above list that it is not always negative. For example, "transitory" has a significantly more positive meaning than "vanity." Something can pass quickly, such as taking a breath, but it is certainly not vain, for without it one would die.

Importantly, the word *hebel* appears multiple times outside of the book of Ecclesiastes and in those occurrences the Septuagint

1 The terms "pre-modern" and "modern" are used to refer to time periods, not philosophical systems.

2 See Sidney Jellicoe, *The Septuagint and Modern Study* (Ann Arbor, MI: Eisenbrauns, 1978), 158–224; Ernst Würthwein, *The Text of the Old Testament: An Introduction to the Biblica Hebraica* (2nd Revised and Enlarged ed.; trans. Erroll F. Rhodes; Grand Rapids, MI: Eerdmans, 1998), 51–52.

3 Würthwein, *The Text of the Old Testament*, 51–52.

translators used a variety of words to translate the word into Greek. For example, they translated Job 7:16 with *kenos*, which means "empty" or "void"; they translated Isaiah 57:13 with *kataigis*, which means "blast of air"; they translated Jeremiah 16:19 with *eidola*, which means "idol"; and they translated Psalm 39:6 (Greek 38:7) with *maten*, which means "in vain." The choice to translate each of these different occurrences of *hebel* outside of Ecclesiastes demonstrates that the word could be translated multiple ways. However, the choice to use only one word to translate every occurrence of *hebel* in Ecclesiastes shows that they understood the word to have a basic consistency or unity within the book. Furthermore, the choice of a word with a broad range of meaning (*mataiotes*) shows that the translators understood that *hebel* could be used in a variety of ways within the book itself. The Septuagint translation thus testifies to the unity and diversity of *hebel* in Ecclesiastes.

Targum

The Targum is a commentary on the Old Testament/Hebrew Bible written by Jewish rabbis. It contains a translation of the Hebrew text in Aramaic as well as a running commentary on the text. It uses two different Aramaic words to translate the Hebrew term *hebel*: *hebel* ("vapor," "breath"; Eccl 1:2 and 2:17) and *hebelo* ("vanity"; all other occurrences). Its first use of "breath" to translate *hebel* is keeping with its interpretive framework, which is "to use the book of Ecclesiastes to fill in gaps in the life of Solomon. . . . Thus, Ecclesiastes became the witness to his return to orthodoxy at the end of his life."[1] In the commentary on Ecclesiastes 1:2, the Targum's commentary relates that Solomon is lamenting the destruction of the temple and Jerusalem—its destruction indicates that all of his labor was "vapor" or "breath" because it did not last for eternity.

1 Longman, *Ecclesiastes*, 3.

Midrash Rabbah Ecclesiastes

Another ancient Jewish commentary, *Midrash Rabbah Ecclesiastes*, translates the term *hebel* as "breath," but understands the word to communicate insubstantiality. By way of explaining the word's meaning, *Midrash Rabbah Ecclesiastes* states, "It may be likened to a man who sets on the fire seven pots one on top of the other, and the steam from the topmost one has no substance in it, [and such is man]."[1] This is an important step in the translation of the book because it unites the word's basic meaning of "breath" with the more metaphorical meaning of "insubstantial."

Jerome

As far as Christian interpretation of Ecclesiastes is concerned, Jerome's translation has had the most significant and lasting impact on how *hebel* has been understood. Jerome's famous translation, the Latin *Vulgate*, was completed in the late fourth/early fifth centuries A.D. Jerome chose to use the term *vanitas* to translate *hebel*. This is an important step in the history of translation because, like the English word "vanity," *vanitas* has a much narrower range of meaning than either *hebel* or the Greek word *mataiotes*.[2] Jerome's translation and commentary popularized what is known as the *contemptis mundi* ("contempt of the world") interpretation of Ecclesiastes.[3] Essentially, the *contemptis mundi* interpretation holds that everything on earth lacks value (i.e. is "vain" or "vanity"). This reading of Ecclesiastes came to dominate Christian scholarship in the Middle Ages, and continues to be a common way to interpret the book even now.

As is the case now, Jerome was careful to qualify his statements regarding the vanity of everything. *Everything* does not lack value, i.e. everything is not "vanity." Instead, spiritual things carry great value, and the earthly realm also has value since it is God's own

1 A. Cohen, transl., *Midrash Rabbah Ecclesiastes* (3rd ed.; Vol. 8; New York: Soncino, 1983), 4.

2 See Fredericks, *Ecclesiastes*, 46–47.

3 Christianson, *Ecclesiastes through the Centuries*, 100–101.

creation. However, these things pale in comparison to God.[1] This understanding of the message of Ecclesiastes is very similar to that often heard today: Everything is vanity . . . without God. This interpretation of *hebel*—that everything is vanity without God—has much to commend it. After all, it is essentially true. A life lived without a relationship with Jesus Christ is no life at all. However, Qoheleth himself points out many things that do indeed have value, such as working, eating, drinking, and one's spouse (Eccl 2:24; 9:9). By offering exceptions to his statement that "everything is *hebel*" he indicates to us that things in this life indeed do have value. Qoheleth is only concerned that we enjoy these gifts of God within the parameters that God has given (Eccl 12:13–14).

Jerome's *vanitas* translation of *hebel* remained dominant throughout the rest of the pre-modern period. However, there were a few scholars who disagreed with Jerome's insistence that all material things were "vanity." For example, Bonaventure argued that "the person who despises the world, despises God."[2] Luther followed Bonaventure's lead by arguing that *hebel* refers to people who are unable to enjoy the gifts of God, not the gifts themselves.[3] Despite these voices that argued against the idea that the world lacks all value, it is evident that this interpretation of *hebel* remained dominant for quite some time, even until now in many circles. However, the modern period brought about a great divergence of opinion regarding how *hebel* is to be understood.

---

1 Ibid. See also K. Farmer, *Who Knows What is Good? A Commentary on the Books of Proverbs and Ecclesiastes* (International Theological Commentary; Grand Rapids, MI: Eerdmans, 1991), 144.

2 St. Bonaventure, *St. Bonaventure's Commentary on Ecclesiastes* (ed. and trans. R. J. Karris and C. Murray; Works of St. Bonaventure VII; Bonaventure, NY: Franciscan, 2005), 77.

3 Martin Luther, *Notes on Ecclesiastes* (ed. and trans. J. Pelikan; Luther's Works 15; St. Louis: Concordia, 1972), 10–11.

Modern Period

Interpreters in the modern era can be arranged on a scale that moves from a negative understanding of *hebel* on one end to a positive understanding of the word on the other. The more positive renderings include literal translations such as "breath" and "vapor" as well as metaphorical terms such as "mystery," "enigma," "beyond mortal grasp," and "transient." I have called these "more positive translations" because they do not immediately call to mind things that are inherently negative. More negative translations include terms such as "meaningless" and "absurd." These translations are labeled "more negative" because they require that the reader understand the message of Ecclesiastes in inherently negative terms.

More Positive Translations

C. L. Seow has argued that *hebel* means "beyond mortal grasp," a translation hearkens back to the literal meaning of the term, "breath" or "vapor." [1] Thus, Qoheleth is arguing that the things he deems *hebel* are those things that are simply outside the reach of humanity. In the same way that one cannot literally hold a breath in one's hand, one cannot grasp the things of which Qoheleth speaks.

Craig Bartholomew has a similar take on the word, arguing that it should be translated as "enigmatic."[2] In his view Qoheleth speaks of issues that are difficult to understand—enigmas. However, Bartholomew also notes that the reader must be attuned to the metaphorical nature of *hebel*: it is a live metaphor, so its meaning must be determined by its surrounding context.[3] Graham Ogden has also translated *hebel* with the terms "enigma" and "mystery."[4] His take on the word is similar to that of Seow because for Ogden the mysterious aspect of the world stems from humanity's inability

1 C. L. Seow, "Beyond Mortal Grasp: The Usage of *Hebel* in Ecclesiastes," *Australian Biblical Review* 48 (2000): 1–16.

2 Bartholomew, *Ecclesiastes*, 106.

3 Ibid.

4 Graham Ogden, "Vanity It Certainly is Not," *The Bible Translator* 38 (1987): 301–307.

to understand everything that goes on around them. These translations of *hebel* are important because enigmas and mysteries are not necessarily negative, so Bartholomew and Ogden allow the reader to determine whether or not Qoheleth's use of *hebel* should be understood negatively.

Daniel Fredericks argues that *hebel* should be translated with the term "transient" or "brief," again relying on the word's literal definition instead of its broader, more metaphorical meanings. In a short book on the meaning of *hebel* in Ecclesiastes, he argues that everything that Qoheleth deems *hebel* is not vain or meaningless; instead, those things are *transient*, soon to disappear. In Fredericks's view, this makes Ecclesiastes an eminently important book for living out a relationship with God, for it forces believers to enjoy the gifts of God while they can, but also to trust in God because the bad times also are fleeting.[1]

These four scholars represent the view that *hebel* should be translated with a more positive—or at least neutral—term. By using a term that does not immediately evoke negative thoughts and feelings, they allow readers to make their own value judgments regarding Qoheleth's *hebel*-statements.

More Negative Translations

As much as the previous scholars allow for a more positive reading of Qoheleth's message, there are other scholars who argue that the book is a largely pessimistic work, which leads them to translate *hebel* with words that communicate the book's supposed pessimism to the modern reader. At the heart of the following translations is the conviction that Ecclesiastes has a bleak outlook on life and often believes God to be distant and unapproachable.

Michael Fox has argued forcefully that *hebel* is best translated by the word "absurd."[2] Fox bases this translation on a comparison

---

1 See Daniel C. Fredericks, *Coping with Transience: Ecclesiastes on Brevity in Life* (The Biblical Seminar 18; Sheffield, England: JSOT Press, 1993).
2 Michael V. Fox, "The Meaning of *Hebel* for Qoheleth," *Journal of Biblical Literature* 105 (1986): 409–27.

between Ecclesiastes and *The Myth of Sisyphus*, a twentieth-century existential work by the famous philosopher Albert Camus. In *The Myth of Sisyphus*, Camus uses the term "absurd" to describe a situation in which the rational relationship between legitimate expectations and outcomes is non-existent, a sentiment that Fox rightly believes Qoheleth shares. However, Fox sees the entire book of Ecclesiastes in a negative light, which is not necessarily the case. He bases his assessment on what he sees as a "crisis" in the wisdom tradition of ancient Israel. In Fox's opinion, the wisdom teachers have grown weary of the type of wisdom in Proverbs, which indicates that certain actions will produce certain results: evil deeds yield punishment, while good deeds yield rewards. I concur that Qoheleth is grappling with this very issue, but disagree that his outlook on life is marred by pessimism. Instead, Qoheleth offers his readers a way to deal with the apparent breakdown between actions and their expected outcomes. I will explore Qoheleth's solution to this problem more in the following lessons.

Tremper Longman is the best representative of those scholars who render *hebel* with the term "meaningless." Longman rightly points out that the term "vanity" is no longer a viable option for translating *hebel* because "the English term 'vanity' is primarily used in reference to self-pride."[1] Longman gets to the heart of the issue for translating *hebel* when he points out that the word's meaning must be determined by its surrounding context, but the word is essential to understanding both the context in which it appears and the book's theological message as a whole. In Longman's view, a robust study of textual criticism, philology (the study of language), and the theology of Ecclesiastes demonstrates that the book is primarily pessimistic. Thus, Longman opts for the word "meaningless" and argues that Qoheleth "leaves nothing out. He cannot find meaning in anybody or anything."[2]

In the final section of this lesson we will show that the meaning of *hebel* is tied closely to the narrative of the world's first murder:

---

1 Longman, *Ecclesiastes*, 61.

2 Ibid., 65.

Cain and Abel. Abel's name is literally "hebel"—the very word used by Ecclesiastes to discuss the various things in life that disturb him. There are certain features that mark Abel's life, such as brevity and injustice, that also mark the issues about which Qoheleth opines. In a course on Ecclesiastes, N. Blake Hearson suggested this connection to me based on the linguistic similarity between *hebel* and Abel and because Abel's death illustrates the injustice that Qoheleth laments. I gratefully acknowledge Hearson's suggestion and the invitation to explore the connection further, which has culminated in the examination of the relationship between *hebel* and Abel in this lesson. Beyond the association between Qoheleth's use of *hebel* and its use in Genesis, there are several passages in Ecclesiastes that indicate the author is intentionally borrowing words and phrases from Genesis in order to link his work to that book. We turn now to the concept of inner-biblical exegesis in order to demonstrate its usefulness for understanding the meaning of *hebel* in Ecclesiastes. We will then show the various places in which Qoheleth borrows from Genesis, and finally we will show how the life of Abel is a test-case for Qoheleth's theological message.

What is Inner-Biblical Exegesis, and Why Does it Matter?

Having surveyed various approaches to translating *hebel* in Ecclesiastes, we now turn to the study of inner-biblical exegesis to see if it can shed light on the meaning of this enigmatic term. Inner-biblical exegesis is a fancy term for something that Bible readers have been doing for quite some time: looking at other verses in the Bible that are connected to the verse one is studying. For most people this means using the column of references that appears on the pages of many Bibles. For example, if I look up Mark 2:18 in my NIV Bible, the reference list in the center column tells me to look at Matthew 6:16–18 and Acts 13:2. The editors of this edition of the Bible think that these other two passages are related in some way to Mark 2:18, so they point me to those texts as well. For the present study, inner-biblical exegesis is important because it is the method by which the author of Ecclesiastes framed his own discussion of life. In what follows I will outline the basic method for determining when Qoheleth is using Genesis as a starting point.

A Method for Determining Inner-Biblical Exegesis

The process for determining the relationship between Genesis and Ecclesiastes is quite similar to the center-column reference method, but with a minor difference. When looking at the relationship between biblical passages by using the center-column reference, one does not generally think about which passage was written first. In our study of Ecclesiastes, we are working on the assumption that Genesis was penned long before Ecclesiastes. While many scholars disagree with this assessment, there is also good reason to hold to Mosaic authorship of the Pentateuch.[1] That Genesis was written first is important because we will be demonstrating how the author of Ecclesiastes has used the first few chapters of Genesis to frame his own discussion of how to get along in a world in which so many things are unjust and unexpected.

Beginning with the assumption that Genesis was written prior to Ecclesiastes, we then use two criteria to determine if a passage in Ecclesiastes alludes to a passage in Genesis. First, there must be a correspondence in themes between the two passages.[2] That is, the thematic elements in the content of Ecclesiastes must be related to the thematic elements in the content of Genesis. For example, if a passage in Ecclesiastes is discussing a theme such as the frustration brought about by death, then that theme must also be present in

---

1 The discussion regarding the date and authorship of the Pentateuch is not appropriate here. However, those interested should look at Sailhammer, *The Meaning of the Pentateuch*, for a defense of Mosaic authorship. The classic volume arguing against Mosaic authorship is Julius Wellhausen, *Prolegomena to the History of Ancient Israel*, which is now available in many different editions.

2 See Michael Fishbane, *Biblical Interpretation in Ancient Israel* (Oxford: Oxford University Press, 1985), 285.

the passage in Genesis. If it is not present, then it would be wrong to assert that Ecclesiastes has borrowed that theme from Genesis.

A second element that is used to determine whether or not Ecclesiastes relies on Genesis is the correspondence of words and phrases. This aspect of inner-biblical exegesis becomes a bit trickier because it requires the use of the original languages. However, this can be done by those who do not know Hebrew with the use of Bible software such as Logos or BibleWorks. This aspect of inner-biblical exegesis is important because the use of identical words indicates that the author was likely intentionally referring to a previous biblical passage. So, if Ecclesiastes uses the term "garden" in a passage that discusses a theme that is also found in a passage in Genesis that uses the word "garden" then it is highly likely that Qoheleth is referring to the text in Genesis. The greater the frequency of repeated words, the more certain that the reader can be regarding Qoheleth's use of Genesis. One caveat is in order here: words often have an overlap in meaning. Therefore, the author of Ecclesiastes may use a *similar* word to describe a particular theme, which indicates that the occurrence of identical words is not necessarily essential to determine borrowing.

The Use of Genesis in Ecclesiastes

By using the guidelines above, we can point to several places in Ecclesiastes where Qoheleth refers to the book of Genesis. The individual occurrence of each of these instances of borrowing does not in itself *prove* that Qoheleth used the book of Genesis; however, when taken as a whole the weight of evidence indicates that Qoheleth intentionally used Genesis to develop his own treatise.

God's Garden

In an article published twenty years ago, Arian Verheij argued that Ecclesiastes 2:4–6 borrowed language from Genesis that describes the Garden of Eden.[1] In Genesis 2:8–10 we read of God's creation of the Garden of Eden:

> And the LORD God planted a garden in Eden, in the east, and there he put the man whom he had formed. And out of the ground the LORD God made to spring up every tree that is pleasant to the sight and good for food. The tree of life was in the midst of the garden, and the tree of the knowledge of good and evil. A river flowed out of Eden to water the garden, and there it divided and became four rivers.

The repetition of terms is striking as Qoheleth describes his building project:

> I made great works. I built houses and planted vineyards for myself. I made myself gardens and parks, and planted in them all kinds of fruit trees. I made myself pools from which to water the forest of growing trees.

In a mere three verses Qoheleth employs eight words that are used in Genesis to describe the Garden of Eden. When Qoheleth "plants" vineyards for himself, it calls to mind God's "planting" of the Garden of Eden in Genesis 2:8. Qoheleth's "gardens" in Ecclesiastes 2:5 call to mind God's garden in Genesis 2:8, 9, 10, 15, and 16. The "fruit trees of every kind" that Qoheleth puts in his own gardens remind us of the same word that appears in Genesis several times (1:11, 12, 29; 2:9, and 16) to describe both the whole of creation and the Garden of Eden itself. Qoheleth "waters" his garden with an irrigation system that reminds the reader of God's "watering" the Garden of Eden (Gen 2:10). Finally, Qoheleth "made" gardens and pools for himself, which is the same term that Genesis uses to describe how God both completed all of the work he had "made" and rested from the work he "made" (Gen 2:2).

The importance of Qoheleth's use of the Garden of Eden material is difficult to overstate because it plays a key role in his overall theology. Qoheleth compares his own building project to God's

---

1 Arian Verheij, "Paradise Retried: On Qoheleth 2:4–6," *Journal for the Study of the Old Testament* 50 (1991): 113–15.

building project, declaring that his (Qoheleth's) work is *hebel*, that is, Abel-like.[1] God's efforts are always good and his work is eternal, but human efforts are riddled with the effects of sin, most clearly demonstrated in the life of Abel. Qoheleth's efforts at replicating God's Garden are bound to dissipate much like Abel's life dissipated far before his time. We will further explore the importance of Qoheleth's efforts to recreate the Garden of Eden in lesson five.

Enjoying God's Good Gifts

Another important aspect of Genesis that Ecclesiastes picks up on is the impetus to enjoy the gifts that God has given. Qoheleth's encouragement to enjoy God's gifts call to mind life before sin, life in the Garden of Eden. No less than six times does he tell his readers to enjoy either food, work, drink, or one's spouse.[2] These four aspects of life—the brief gifts God has given us to enjoy—represent a significant part of existence in the Garden.

Genesis 2:15 states that God created man and placed him in the Garden to work it and keep it. God then gave Adam the freedom to eat from any of the trees in the Garden; next he created a companion suitable for Adam so that he would not be alone in the Garden. The Garden of Eden was a place for enjoying food, drink, work, and one's spouse (and of course the presence of God). Here, in the pre-sin world, humanity was able to enjoy fully the gifts of God.

The six so-called *carpe diem* passages (Eccl 2:24–26; 3:10–22; 5:17–19; 8:10–15; 9:7–10; 11:7–10) call to mind this time in the Garden of Eden with a repetition of words and phrases used in Genesis. Five of the passages in Ecclesiastes use the Hebrew word for man, *adam*; four use the term "eat"; one refers to a man's "wife"; and every one of them uses the term "good," which is a key word that Genesis uses to describe life in the Garden. Finally,

---

1 I am indebted to N. Blake Hearson for the idea that "Abel-like" or "Abel-ness" would be an appropriate translation for the term hebel.

2 Eccl 2:24–26; 3:10–22; 5:17–19; 8:10–15; 9:7–10; 11:7–10.

the thematic element of work, or vocation, is combined with the theme of enjoyment to describe the way that life should be lived. God created humanity, placed them in a good place and gave them good gifts to enjoy. Qoheleth beckons his readers to return to this type of lifestyle, a life characterized by enjoyment of God's good gifts. We will look more closely at the relationship between Ecclesiastes and the Garden of Eden in lesson five, where we examine Qoheleth's call to joy.

From Dust, and Back to Dust

The 1662 *Book of Common Prayer* records the well-known phrase often spoken at funerals: "ashes to ashes, dust to dust." This phrase comes from the book of Genesis where God pronounces the curse on Adam and Eve after they have sinned by eating of the forbidden tree: "By the sweat of your face you shall eat bread, till you return to the ground, for out of it you were taken; for you are dust, and to dust you shall return" (Gen 3:19). Qoheleth repeats this sentiment twice, first in chapter three and again in chapter twelve. In the first instance (Eccl 3:19–20) Qoheleth is discussing the frustration he feels because humans and animals share the same fate:

> For what happens to the children of man and what happens to the beasts is the same; as one dies, so dies the other. They all have the same breath and man has no advantage over the beast, for all is *hebel.* All go to one place. All are from the dust, and to dust all return.

The phrase occurs again at the end of Qoheleth's famous poem on death and dying. He states, "and the dust returns to the earth as it was, and the spirit returns to God who gave it . . ." (Eccl 12:7). Qoheleth uses this language from Genesis to discuss the brevity of human life and the fact that we all meet the same end: death. This is a key topic in Ecclesiastes and will be discussed fully in lesson three.

The final aspect of inner-biblical exegesis that we will discuss is Qoheleth's use of the term *hebel*, which is the name given to the world's first murder victim, Abel. However, before examining the relationship between *hebel* and Abel, it is important to outline briefly the narrative of Cain and Abel in order to explore how the Qoheleth uses the word.

Cain, Abel, and the Meaning of Hebel in Ecclesiastes

After Adam and Eve sinned against God and were banished from the Garden of Eden, it appeared that things could not get much worse. Only one chapter later we learn that things have gotten much, much worse as sin crouches at Cain's door and he refuses to overcome it, choosing instead to slay his own brother because Abel offered to the Lord an acceptable sacrifice. Sin had entered the world through Cain's parents and was now in full bloom in his own life.

An interesting difference between Adam's and Eve's sin and Cain's sin quickly presents itself in the narrative, a difference that has caused consternation since. When Adam and Eve sinned, the consequences were nearly immediate: they realized their nakedness, felt shame, then were expelled from God's Garden where they experienced suffering, pain, and strenuous work (Gen 3:14–19). The right order of the world—sin and punishment—was clear. Adam and Eve sinned, and Adam and Eve suffered the consequences of their sin. However, when Cain sinned, it was Abel the righteous who suffered. When Cain sinned, Abel's life was ended before he could experience the blessing that was thought to be a sign of righteousness: wealth, children, and a long life.

Cain certainly suffered to some degree, as God himself said, "And now you are cursed from the ground, which has opened its mouth to receive your brother's blood from your hand. When you work the ground, it shall no longer yield to you its strength. You shall be a fugitive and a wanderer on the earth" (Gen 4:11–12). However, upon God's pronouncement of cursing, Cain protests, stating, "My punishment is greater than I can bear. Behold, you have driven me today away from the ground, and from your face I shall be hidden. I shall be a fugitive and a wanderer on the earth, and whoever finds me will kill me" (Gen 4:13–14). The Lord relents by placing a mark of protection on Cain that assures him that he will not suffer the same fate he had determined for his righteous brother. The text then relates that Cain does indeed leave the Lord's presence, but God allows him to live a long life that includes building great cities, amassing wealth, and having multiple children—the very things that would mark a righteous person's life.

Whereas Adam and Eve experienced a one-to-one relationship between suffering and disobedience, the opposite is true in the narrative of Cain and Abel. The relationship between righteousness and blessing, disobedience and cursing, has been broken. It is this breakdown between actions and consequences, the oppressive nature of death, and the overwhelming brevity of life that Ecclesiastes explores to great extent by using the term *hebel*, the very name of Abel, the person who provides the most concrete example of these three aspects of life. At the beginning and end of Ecclesiastes the author states that everything is *hebel*, that is, everything reflects Abel in some way. In the following lessons we will explore the various ways that the book of Ecclesiastes uses the term *hebel* ("Abel") to reflect on life on earth and how followers of God should respond to the injustices experienced on this side of heaven.

Conclusion

The meaning of *hebel* is crucial to the meaning of Ecclesiastes. We saw in this lesson that the word has been understood variously throughout history and that the dominant translation, "vanity," came to the fore as a result of Jerome's translation so many centuries ago. We also saw that this is not an accurate translation for today because "vanity" has a much more limited range of meaning than the Hebrew word *hebel*. In order to move beyond this term, I proposed that we should understand *hebel* in relationship to the name of Abel, the world's first murder victim. The Hebrew word used for Abel's name is the same word that Qoheleth uses to describe life as he experienced it and as we often experience it. In order to support Qoheleth's use of the Cain and Abel narrative, we looked at the various ways in which he uses the technique of inner-biblical exegesis to tie his writing to the book of Genesis. The multiple ties to Genesis, along with the strong thematic unity between Abel's life and Ecclesiastes's discussion of life has led us to the conclusion that a strong relationship exists between the two. In the following lessons we will look more closely at Qoheleth's use of *hebel* and the comparisons that can be made to the life of Abel. These comparisons will clarify the meaning and message of Ecclesiastes in a way that allows us to hear and apply the book today.

Discussion Questions

1. We discussed several different options for the meaning of *hebel* in Ecclesiastes. How do the different options change the way you read the book as a whole?

2. Does learning the history of interpretation of the word *hebel* change your view of the book in any way? How? Why?

3. We looked at several ways that the book of Ecclesiastes "echoes" the book of Genesis. Have you used the center column in your Bible in the past to look at what different passages say about the same issues? How is looking at the relationship between Genesis and Ecclesiastes similar to and different from that practice? Has seeing those connections changed the way that your read Ecclesiastes? In what way?

4. What aspects of life have you experienced that reflect the life of Abel? What things in your life would cause you to say "this is *hebel*"? Does reading the word *hebel* as "Abel-like" change the meaning of the book in any significant way?

Lesson Three

Objective: Upon completion of this lesson, you will have a clear understanding of the role of death in Ecclesiastes. This knowledge of the role of death in the book as a whole help you to have a more complete understanding of the book's purpose and its place in the Christian life. More so, understanding the brevity of life and inevitability of death will allow you to apply the book's message to your own life in a meaningful way because each of us must grapple with the fact that our lives end all too quickly.

Opening Prayer: Dear God, thank you for your grace and goodness, and for the opportunity to engage in studying your Word. I pray that you would guide my studies today so you receive glory and I become more like you. As I read the book of Ecclesiastes, may your Word pierce my heart and change my life. May your kingdom come and your will be done on earth as it is in heaven. In Jesus's name, Amen.

Weekly Reading: Once again, this week we will read the entire book of Ecclesiastes. However, since you've been reading the book every day for the past two weeks, you already have a good understanding of the book's flow and the author's thought process. This week you will only need to read two chapters each day. Since there are only twelve chapters, this leaves you an extra day in case you have to miss a reading. You will also be reading several individual passages in the book as we work through this week's discussion of Ecclesiastes's view of death.

Lesson Outline:

1. The problem of brevity in the book of Genesis
2. The problem of brevity in the book of Ecclesiastes

3. The problem of brevity in our lives today

Introduction

Last week we determined that Qoheleth used the book of Genesis at several points in his own work. The importance of Qoheleth's use of Genesis is that it helps us to understand the book of Ecclesiastes more fully, and therefore apply it to our lives more faithfully. One of the most important aspects of our study of Ecclesiastes's inner-biblical exegesis is the light that it sheds on the meaning of Ecclesiastes's key word, *hebel*. In this lesson we will continue to discuss the meaning of *hebel*, but more specifically how Qoheleth uses the word to discuss the one aspect of life that confronts everyone (except Elijah and Enoch!): death. In order to examine Qoheleth's view of death, we will begin by looking at how the first four chapters of Genesis deal with death. We will then look at the passages in Ecclesiastes that discuss death. Finally, lest we become too morbid, we will look briefly at how Ecclesiastes encourages us to cope with life's transience. Our discussion in this lesson will provide a better foundation for understanding the importance of enjoying God's gifts and trusting in his sovereignty, which are the topics for lessons five and six.

The Problem of Brevity in the Book of Genesis

Adam and Eve: Sin and Death Enter the World

The book of Genesis begins with a magnificent display of God's creative powers as he creates the world and extends his lovingkindness to the world's first couple: Adam and Eve. He places them in the Garden of Eden, a place where all their needs are met, where they have fellowship with God, and where they can experience the pleasures of life such as eating, drinking, working, and communing with one another. Life is perfect. However, as we know all too well, this perfection was not to last, for the serpent soon came to Eve to tempt her, saying, "Did God actually say, 'You shall not eat of any tree in the garden'?" (Gen 3:1). With this one small question, Satan has opened the door for Eve to sin against God. As Bruce Waltke states, "The practical effect [of Satan's question] is to hook Eve into a dialogue that opens her mind to a whole new realm of possibility. Satan has no advantage over Eve or us until he diverts our attention with the possibility of disobeying."[1] We all know, as did both Eve and Satan, that God had not forbidden Adam and Eve from eating from every tree in the Garden of Eden, but only one—the tree of the knowledge of good and evil. However, Eve allowed Satan to cause her to "focus on the forbidden thing rather than on God's true blessings," which in turn led her to disobey God.[2] This one small act—eating a piece of fruit—threw open the doors of sin and death has reigned in our world ever since.

We may think that the punishment was far too great for such a small crime. However, we must remember a few things about life in the Garden. First, God had already warned Adam and Eve that when they eat from the forbidden tree, they "shall surely die" (Gen 2: 17). Second, God gave specific instructions to Adam and Eve and placed them in a perfect environment where they had a vibrant, continual relationship with the Creator of the universe. Third, the act of eating the fruit from the tree of the knowledge of good and evil was more than just eating forbidden fruit. By eating the forbidden fruit Adam and Eve were proclaiming their own autonomy, declaring that they were gods, not creatures.[3] Their act of defiance resulted in spiritual death—alienation from God—and later physical death.

---

1 Bruce Waltke, *An Old Testament Theology: An Exegetical, Canonical, and Thematic Approach* (Grand Rapids, MI: Zondervan, 2007), 261.

2 Ibid., 262.

3 Ibid., 263.

Cain and Abel: The Escalation of Sin and Death in the World

After expulsion from the Garden and severance of their perfect relationship with God, Adam and Eve continue to live out their lives. They settle east of Eden and Adam begins to work the ground with great effort, while he and Eve try to work out their relationship in light of their new sin nature. They have children, first Cain and then Abel. These two sons have knowledge of God, for each of them brings to the Lord a sacrifice from his respective line of work. Cain is an agriculturalist who, like Adam, works the ground for his sustenance. Cain brought to the Lord an offering "of the fruit of the ground" (Gen 4:3), while Abel brought to the Lord an offering "of the firstborn of his flock and of their fat portions" (Gen 4:4). Genesis then goes on to tell us that the Lord "had regard for Abel and his offering, but for Cain and his offering he had no regard" (Gen 4:4–5).

Scholars have long debated exactly why God accepted Abel's offering and rejected Cain's. Hermann Gunkel argued that God simply prefers shepherds over famers, but this is unlikely because God later gives prescriptions for how to worship him with the fruits of agriculture.[1] Claus Westermann posited that God rejected Cain's sacrifice just because he wanted; there was no qualitative difference between the two sacrifices, and it would have been impossible for Cain to know in advance that God would disapprove of his sacrifice.[2] This view is also unlikely because even from the beginning God made clear his requirements for obedience. God does not hide in the shadows, making us guess what will please him and what will not. One of the beauties of worshiping the Lord as opposed to other gods in the ancient Near East is that he is forthcoming concerning how to be in right relationship with him. Gerhard von Rad thought that Cain's sacrifice was rejected because it did not come

1 Hermann Gunkel, *Genesis* (trans. Mark E. Biddle; Mercer Library of Biblical Studies; Macon, GA: Mercer University Press, 1997), 43.

2 Claus Westermann, *Genesis 1–11* (Continental Commentary; trans. John J. Scullion; Minneapolis, MN: Fortress, 1997), 296.

with blood.[1] But, as Waltke points out, the Old Testament makes plenty of room for sacrifices that do not require blood (e.g. Lev 2:4; 1 Sam 10:27; 1 Kgs 10:25).[2] What, then, is the issue with Cain's sacrifice? Again Bruce Waltke is helpful on this issue. The Lord "had no regard" for Cain's sacrifice because Cain gave it in half-heartedly. Whereas Abel gave from the "firstborn" of his flock, Cain simply offered "the fruit of the ground" (Gen 4:3). Abel "scented his tribute with the incense of love, faith, and devotion," but Cain offered out of a sense of "tokenism," a type of religion devoid of any real sense of relationship or devotion to the Lord.[3] The issue at stake regarding these two sacrifices is the attitude of the giver. Waltke also points out that this narrative is highly instructive for us today as we seek to live in right relationship with God: "Unless we offer our best to God, our sacrifice is a stench in his nostrils."[4]

That Cain's heart and attitude were the issue in God's rejecting Cain's offering becomes clearer when we read how the events continued to unfold. At the Lord's rejection, Cain became "very angry, and his face fell" (Gen 4:5). God demonstrates his grace toward Cain by reaching out to him, assuring Cain that he would accept his offering if he would only "do well" (Gen 4:7). However, Cain does not do well; instead, he lashes out in anger, murdering his brother Abel in a fit of jealousy. Death entered into the world when Adam and Eve sinned against God by eating from the tree of the knowledge of good and evil. However, Adam and Eve did not suffer immediate, physical death. When Cain murdered Abel, he forced his family to experience the full force of physical death for the first time, and people today still struggle to cope with the brevity of human life.

Abel lived an all-too-brief life. According to the biblical witness, Abel was a righteous person who followed the Lord (Matt

1 Gerhard von Rad, *A Commentary on Genesis* (trans. Ford L. Battles; Library of Christian Classics 20; Philadelphia: Westminster, 1972), 104.
2 Waltke, *Old Testament Theology*, 270.
3 Ibid.
4 Ibid.

25:35). However, rather than being awarded for his faithfulness to God, he suffered death at the hands of a jealous brother whom sin had overtaken (Gen 4:7). He was unable to experience any of the rewards that the godly person could expect: long life, many children, and provision (see, for example Deut 7:11–14; 30:11–20). Instead, Abel experienced the rewards of the wicked: a brief life, barrenness, and lack of provision (see Duet 18:15–68). The primary issue that we will focus on in this lesson is Abel's brief life, for it is life's brevity—exemplified by death—that preoccupies the writer of Ecclesiastes.

The Problem of Brevity in the Book of Ecclesiastes

Qoheleth examines many aspects of life in an effort to live a life of faith in a world that constantly attacks his faith in the Lord. Over and over again Qoheleth laments the fact that death comes to every person, whether righteous or unrighteous. He senses that death is unnatural and that its all-encompassing, unforgiving nature is inherently unjust. Using the key word *hebel*, the same word used to name the person who first tasted physical death, Qoheleth discusses the injustice of life's brevity, which the pervasiveness of death makes abundantly clear. In this section we will work through the passages in which Qoheleth uses the term *hebel* to describe situations in life that reflect the "Abel-ness" of life in the sense of brevity and the injustice that accompanies death. By working through theses passages we will see that Qoheleth connects many aspects of life to the injustice of death that Abel suffered.

Excursus: Ecclesiastes 1:2 and 12:8

Before delving into the passages that deal with life's brevity, we must first look at what scholars often refer to as the book's "frame."[1] Ecclesiastes 1:2 and 12:8 repeat the same words: "*Hebel* of *hebels*, says the preacher, *hebel* of *hebels*. Everything is *hebel*." (We

---

1 See, for example, Longman, *Ecclesiastes*, 58–59.

discovered in the previous lesson that most words used to translate the term *hebel* do not adequately convey what Qoheleth is talking about, which is why I have chosen to leave it untranslated throughout this study guide.) Qoheleth uses these two statements to set the tone for his work: everything in some way reflects the life of Abel.

It is important to note here that Qoheleth is not necessarily talking about everything that has ever existed; instead, he is using a literary device called hyperbole—overstatement for effect.[1] He is using the term "everything" to refer "primarily to things mentioned in the immediate context" as a way to draw the reader into his story.[2] Imagine if a friend is recounting his experience at an exciting basketball game and says "Everyone was going crazy!" Now, we know that it is highly unlikely that "everyone" was "going crazy." We understand that our friend means that the people in the stands were actively involved in the exciting game. In the same way, when Qoheleth uses the term "everything" he is using it to point to the things that he is talking about in his treatise. So, when he says that everything in life is *hebel*—that everything in some way reflects the life of Abel—we should understand that he is talking about specific things, such as human existence, work, injustice, and even life's pleasures. All of these things in some way reflect the life of Abel.

Another key to understanding Qoheleth's message is understanding what he means by *hebel*. In the previous lesson we learned that most modern translations use words to translate *hebel* that do not carry the same meaning that the original Hebrew word carried. We also learned that Ecclesiastes makes frequent use of the book of Genesis, which led us to the conclusion that Qoheleth's use of *hebel* was no mere coincidence. Qoheleth uses this specific word to call to mind specific aspects of Abel's life, which he then uses to examine

---

1 Michael V. Fox argues that Qoheleth does in fact mean "all," but that he qualifies it with "in the world" (Michael V. Fox, *A Time to Tear Down and a Time to Build Up: A Rereading of Ecclesiastes* [Grand Rapids, MI: Eerdmans, 1999], 162.

2 Douglas Miller, *Symbol and Rhetoric in the Book of Ecclesiastes: The Place of Hebel in Qoheleth's Work* (Leiden: Brill, 2002), 99–100.

the same things he sees in his own life, such as life's brevity and the breakdown between actions and expected outcomes.

Moving forward we should examine the book of Ecclesiastes with the book's frame in mind. At the outset, Qoheleth states that everything—that is, everything under discussion—is *hebel*—that is, reflects the life of Abel in some way. Understanding the beginning and concluding statements in this way allows us to interpret properly what Qoheleth is discussing and what he means when he calls it *hebel*. In turn, proper interpretation leads to more faithful application to our own lives, which will allow us to become more like Christ and live in right relationship with him.

The Brevity of Pleasure

We will learn later that Qoheleth commends pleasure in this life because it is one of God's gifts to his creation. However, Qoheleth also laments the fact that pleasure is fleeting. Although we can and should enjoy the good things in life—the things that bring us pleasure—we must also recognize that these things are here today and gone tomorrow. This is both a cause for consternation in Qoheleth's view and the primary reason that we should enjoy *now*: we may not have the opportunity tomorrow.

The first mention of the brevity of pleasure comes in Ecclesiastes 2:1: "I said in my heart, 'Come now, I will test you with pleasure; enjoy yourself.' But behold, this also was *hebel*." Tremper Longman argues that the pleasure to which Qoheleth refers in this verse is "sensual, material joy" that leaves Qoheleth unfulfilled, thus pointing again to the utter meaninglessness of life.[1] However, Daniel Fredericks takes the opposite track, arguing that the type of pleasure in view is not carnal or sinful, but fundamentally transient.[2] We may find some clarification in the next verse in which Qoheleth states, "I said of laughter, 'It is mad,' and of pleasure, 'What use is it?'" (Eccl 2:2). Laughter and pleasure lack value not

1 Longman, *Ecclesiastes*, 88.

2 Fredericks, *Coping with Transience*, 69.

because they are "meaningless," but because they are fleeting, brief, transient—they resemble the life of Abel. Pleasure gives no *ultimate* satisfaction because it does not last. Even though pleasure must not be life's goal, it remains a gift of God. In this verse we learn that pleasure-seeking will leave us unfulfilled. Should we enjoy God's gifts? Yes, but we must be careful not to place too much stock in things that pass so quickly.

Qoheleth drives home the point about pleasure's brevity in 5:10–12:

> He who loves money will not be satisfied with money, nor he who loves wealth with his income; this is also *hebel.* When goods increase, they increase who eat them, and what advantage has their owner but to see them with his eyes? Sweet is the sleep of the laborer, whether he eats little or much, but the full stomach of the rich will not let him sleep.

If we are honest, then we will agree that money has the capacity to bring its owners pleasure. Qoheleth points out in verse 11 that the advantage of wealth and material goods is that the owner can see them with his eyes and thus receive some sort of satisfaction from his wealth. As Fredericks states, "As long as one can enjoy his property, even if only by viewing it and being satisfied with the sight of it, this is *some* advantage (5.11c)."[1]

However, Qoheleth is no fool when it comes to wealth. He states in no uncertain terms that it does not satisfy because it is fleeting. This becomes clear in the following verses where Qoheleth expands on the problems associated with wealth by bringing to mind a story of a man who kept his wealth "to his own hurt" (Eccl 5:13). This person never took the opportunity to enjoy his wealth and indeed lost it suddenly in a "bad venture" (Eccl 5:14). Those of us in the United States who have experienced the economic downturn since 2008 can attest to the fleeting nature of wealth and the dangers associated with amassing it for no good reason. Even in a nation as wealthy as the United States, there are no guarantees that

1 Ibid., 72.

the accrued wealth will remain with us. It is marked by transience; attempting to grasp and hold on to it is a foolish enterprise.

Another aspect of wealth that Qoheleth points out is that as it increases, so do those who want to spend it! Anecdotal stories abound about lottery winners who filed for bankruptcy only a short time after hitting it big. There are certainly many factors that contribute to such a situation, but at least one of those factors is that people come out of the woodworks to befriend a person who has won the lottery: "when goods increase, they increase who eat them." Qoheleth did not have in mind the lottery specifically, and the vast majority of the world is never going to experience sudden wealth. Nevertheless, we may still be able to relate to the way hip-hop artist Notorious B.I.G. framed the sentiment: "mo' money, mo' problems."[1]

The problem with pleasure for Qoheleth is that it does not last. He tested himself with pleasure in chapter 2, only to find that it was Abel-like because it passed too quickly. We find in chapter five that he finds some advantage in wealth—the advantage of seeing it—but that wealth also passes quickly. No one can really hold on to their wealth; like sand, it slips through the fingers. Wealth is not necessarily an evil thing for it truly can bring some modicum of pleasure, but the failure to enjoy that wealth—even if such enjoyment is fleeting—is problematic for Qoheleth. In lesson five we will explore the importance of enjoyment for Qoheleth and find that the fleeting nature of things that bring pleasure is the very reason why we should strive to enjoy God's gifts today.

A final aspect of pleasure that Qoheleth points out as brief is the laughter of fools in 7:6, "For as the crackling of thorns under a pot, so is the laughter of the fools; this also is *hebel*." Please do not mistake the inclusion of this verse in our discussion of pleasure as an endorsement of foolish laughter. Qoheleth is in no way endorsing the laughter of fools as he does other transient gifts that God has given. Instead, he is using the laughter of fools as an example

1 Notorious B.I.G., "Mo Money Mo Problems," *Life after Death* (New York: Bad Boy Records, 1997).

of yet another feature of life that passes quickly. He makes his point clearly by comparing the fool's laughter with "the crackling of thorns under a pot."

My wife and I have a raspberry patch in our backyard that brings us no small delight. It produces a good number of raspberries each year, which we thoroughly enjoy when we are able to harvest them before our two small dogs start snacking on them. The difficult part of the harvesting is avoiding all of those pesky thorns. Avoiding the thorns becomes even more difficult in the fall when I cut back the bushes and burn the trimmings. But, it is quite a sight to see those thorns go up in flames! They catch fire almost immediately, burst into massive flames, then burn out just as quickly. This is what Qoheleth has in mind when he speaks of the laughter of fools. There is no real benefit in burning the thorny parts of the bushes—they burn hotly, but not long enough to cook anything or even keep a person warm for very long. The burning thorns have no substance and the flames pass as quickly as they began. This statement is therefore encouraging, for we know that foolish laughter will pass as quickly as it came.

In this section we saw that one of the primary reasons for enjoying life is that pleasure passes quickly. We must grasp God's gifts *now* because they may not be here tomorrow. At the same time, we saw that some features of pleasure—such as the fool's laugher—are just as fleeting, and in this also we can receive encouragement. We turn now to one of the primary problems for Qoheleth—the fleeting nature of life itself.

The Brevity of Life

We spent a significant amount of time looking at the brevity of life in the book of Genesis. Life's brevity—that is, death—was a cause for concern in that book, and is an even greater cause for concern in Ecclesiastes. Qoheleth introduces his frustration with death early on in Ecclesiastes. After reading through his introduction in Ecclesiastes 1 and his thoughts on the brevity of pleasure, we come upon his first statement regarding death:

> The wise person has eyes in his head, but the fool walks in darkness. And yet I perceived that the same event happens to all of them. Then I said in my heart, "What happens to the fool will happen to me also. Why then have I been so very wise?" And I said in my heart that this also is *hebel*. For of the wise as of the fool there is no enduring remembrance, seeing that in the days to come all will have been long forgotten. How the wise dies just like the fool! So I hated life, because what is done under the sun was grievous to me, for all is *hebel* and a striving after wind. (Eccl 2:14–17)

It is difficult to read these verses and not feel the pain and frustration in Qoheleth's voice. Although he states that there is some advantage in being wise—wise people at least can see!—he also realizes that the same fate is going to overtake both the wise and the foolish. Death comes to all, and there is nothing anyone can do to prevent it. The fact that Qoheleth will be forgotten makes matters worse. As Fredericks points out, "'forgotten' means more than merely not being recollected; it means to be intentionally marginalized out of existence."[1] The concept of "remembering" and "forgetting" is connected to the relational aspect of life.[2] This becomes clear when we look at passages where God "remembers" his people, such as Exodus 2:24. God's remembering his people Israel means that he acts on their behalf because of a prior relationship with them. Thus, while it is true that life passes quickly and there is the distinct possibility that what we do here on earth will vanish with us, what really concerns Qoheleth is that the relational aspect of his life will be "consciously neglected" as is too often the case when we "forget" loved ones as they become older and need our care the most.[3]

---

1 Fredericks, *Ecclesiastes*, 97.

2 Ibid.

3 Ibid.

The transience of life, which is made so much more permanent by the act of forgetting, leads Qoheleth to hate life and everything done under the sun because it is *hebel*, that is, marked by Abel-ness. In this use of the term *hebel* Qoheleth refers to the fact that life ends too early, like Abel's life, but he also hints at the fact that life is often unjust. It is simply not right that the foolish and the wise suffer the same fate, an aspect of Ecclesiastes that we will explore more fully in the following lesson.

We come upon the next statement about life's brevity in Ecclesiastes 3:18–21:

> I said in my heart with regard to the children of man that God is testing them that they may see that they themselves are but beasts. For what happens to the children of man and what happens to the beasts is the same; as one dies so dies the other. They all have the same breath, and man as no advantage over the beasts, for all is *hebel.* All go to one place. All are from the dust, and to dust all return. Who knows whether the spirit of man goes upward and the spirit of the beast goes down into the earth?

This passage—one of the most depressing in Scripture—drives home what frustrates Qoheleth the most: humans and animals alike die. In the previous passage we examined we found that Qoheleth was deeply troubled by the fact that the fool and the wise both die, and here again the lack of differentiation in judgment bothers him. It matters not whether one is foolish or wise, beast or animal, for all are *hebel*—fleeting. If we were at first unsure that Qoheleth here alludes to the transience of life—the aspect of Abel's life made clear by his early departure—then he drives home the point by referring explicitly to the fact that that death is what makes humans and animals the same. Furthermore, he points to the departure of a person's very being: "Who knows whether the spirit of a man goes upward?"

We also saw in the previous lesson that Qoheleth's reference to dust in this passage is one of the ways that he refers the reader back to Genesis, where we first learn that humans came from and will return to the dust. Craig Bartholomew points out that Genesis is abundantly clear that a fundamental difference between humans and animals is that humans are created in God's own image. However, "the common observable fate of both animals and humans raises for Qoheleth the question as to whether there is any difference between them: they all have the same spirit (*rûaḥ*), and its destination is the same."[1] On this side of the cross we know that for those who trust in Christ, "while we are at home in the body we are away from the Lord, for we walk by faith, not by sight. Yes, we are of good courage, and we would rather be away from the body and at home with the Lord" (2 Cor 5:6–8). Therefore, we must not read too much into Qoheleth's declaration, for he is speaking of what he can see with his eyes. In doing so, he demonstrates for believers today an appropriate way to grapple with life's disappointments and mysteries. We may say to God that what we see with our eyes is not at all encouraging, but we also must trust that what he has said in his Word is true. The ability to express frustration can go a long way to alleviate our inner turmoil, and modeling for others how to interact with God in the face of difficult circumstances may go a long way toward discipling them in the faith.

Qoheleth next speaks of life's brevity in 6:3–4, a difficult passage to read:

> If a man fathers a hundred children and lives many years, so that the days of his years are many, but his soul is not satisfied with life's good things, and he has no burial, I say that a stillborn child is better off than he. For it comes in *hebel* and goes in darkness, and in darkness its name is covered. Moreover, it has not seen the sun or known anything, yet it finds rest rather than he. Even though he should live a thousand years twice over, yet enjoy no good—do not all go to the one place?

A stillborn child represents life's transience in a powerful way. Stillborn children are transient to the utmost degree, for they *nev-*

1 Bartholomew, *Ecclesiastes*, 177.

er have the opportunity to experience life.[1] This statement seems strange coming from the lips of Qoheleth, who has decried life's brevity throughout the rest of the book, leaving us to wonder why he thinks a stillborn child is better off than a person who has lived a long life. Tremper Longman points out a connection between Psalm 58:8, in which the psalmist curses his enemies, hoping that they will be "like the stillborn child, who never sees the sun."[2] Even this situation, considered by the psalmist to be such a horrific fate, is preferable to having God's gifts but not being able to enjoy them. Praising death in this way goes against our deepest sensibilities, but is part of Qoheleth's rhetorical strategy. Such a startling statement drives home Qoheleth's view that enjoyment in life is paramount: even being stillborn is preferable to living an interminably long life (2,000 years!)—which also will end—with many blessings that are not enjoyed.

Before we make any decisions about the preferability of death, we must listen to the twinge of resolve in Qoheleth's voice. He is not advocating death over life in all situations, but given the two options—between rest and anxiety—Qoheleth opts for the former. Again, the resolve in this situation highlights the premium that Qoheleth places on the enjoyment of God's gifts. If God allows us to enjoy the gifts he has given, then we must take care to embrace them fully (though, as we will see, we must enjoy them within the appropriate boundaries). Since life is fraught with Abel-ness—in this case transience—we have to take every opportunity to embrace the fleeting gifts of God.

After discussing issues related to the enjoyment of life, Qoheleth returns again to the issue of life's brevity a few verses later: "The more words, the more *hebel* and what is the advantage to man? For who knows what is good for man while he lives the few days of his *hebel* life, which he passes like a shadow? For who can tell man

---

1 Note Miller's discussion of this passage, in which he suggests that Qoheleth may be referring to the vapor that was thought to surround a child during gestation (*Symbol and Rhetoric*, 125–8).

2 Longman, *Ecclesiastes*, 171.

what will be after him under the sun?" (Eccl 6:11–12). Qoheleth brings up two important, related issues in this passage. First, he states that the "more words, the more *hebel*." How are we to treat this statement? Is Qoheleth saying that words increase "vanity"? Remembering that Qoheleth is often preoccupied with life's brevity, Daniel Fredericks's translation is instructive here: "Since there are many things that magnify impermanence."[1] The Hebrew term *debarim* is often translated as "words," but it carries the meaning of "matter, thing" as well. Thus, Fredericks's translation clarifies that Qoheleth is not speaking *only* about the increase of words, but the fact that there are many things in life that increase, or magnify, its brevity. Perhaps Qoheleth was thinking of the quickness with which children grow into adults. Or maybe he was reflecting on his most recent high school reunion? Probably not, but we can all think of events in life that cause that pang of feeling time's passage and make us think deeply about how our lives pass so quickly before us.

The second issue that Qoheleth brings up in this passage is the *hebel* nature of a person's "few days" of life. This use of *hebel* makes it even clearer that Qoheleth is referring to the transient nature of Abel's life, for the use of the words "few" and "shadow" highlight brevity. The comparison of one's life to a shadow is a somewhat common idiom in Hebrew that we see often in the Bible (Job 8:9; 14:2; Pss 102:11; 144:4; 1 Chr 29:15).[2] Finally, Qoheleth has placed *hebel* next to the nouns that precede it with no intervening verb. This is a common grammatical feature of Hebrew that scholars usually translate into English with a helping verb. However, one way to translate this phrase that draws out the verse's implications is, "The few days of his life, that is, his transience." This translation highlights the fact that Qoheleth is drawing our attention to the transitory nature of life. Just like Abel passed quickly from this life into the next, so does every other person. Once again Qoheleth reminds his readers that our days pass like a shadow; our time on this earth is very, very brief.

---

1 Fredericks, *Ecclesiastes*, 164.

2 Ibid., 165.

Before ending his monologue, Qoheleth returns to the issue of life's brevity in 11:8–10:

> So if a person lives many years, let him rejoice in them all; but let him remember that the days of darkness will be many. All that comes is *hebel*. Rejoice, O young man, in your youth, and let your heart cheer you in the days of your youth. Walk in the ways of your heart and the sight of your eyes. But know that for all these things God will bring you into judgment. Remove vexation from your heart, and put away pain from your body, for youth and the dawn of life are *hebel*.

Qoheleth's declaration of Abel-ness in this passage concludes several statements about how to live in this present life. Hearkening back to his earlier discussions of enjoying life, he reminds his readers that they should do all they can to enjoy the life God has given. Like any good teacher, he tempers this reminder with another piece of advice: "let him remember that the days of darkness will be many." The implication is that we should enjoy the good things while we can because there will be many days in which there is no good to enjoy. He follows this reminder with a summary statement about all of life: "all that comes is *hebel*." Everything that we will face in this life is transient. While on earth, there is nothing permanent. For Qoheleth this fact is reason for both rejoicing and lamenting. We should rejoice because we know that the "days of darkness" will pass, but we also lament because we know that our joyful experiences will not last. His final statement regarding life's brevity is an admonition to put away vexation and pain because youth is *hebel*, that is, fleeting. We should not fool ourselves into thinking that we will always be young; rather, while we are young we should strive to enjoy life as much as possible because we know that our time on earth is passing quickly.

The Problem of Brevity in Our Lives Today

We have spent this lesson looking at an issue that is as prevalent today as it was centuries ago when Qoheleth first wrote these words. Qoheleth states in no uncertain terms that life's pleasures, and even life itself, are riddled with the same trouble that plagued Abel: they are fleeting. Abel's life was cut short when his brother jealously murdered him, and while we may not suffer the same sort of end to our lives, we can rest assured that we will indeed taste life's brevity.

Qoheleth's discussion of life's brevity is important for believers today for a few reasons. First, Qoheleth's words provide impetus for us to enjoy the gifts of God. We should understand that the good things in life are not promised to us; they are God's good gifts. Likewise, we should understand that experiencing God's gifts today does not guarantee that we will also experience them tomorrow. This causes us to embrace life's pleasures immediately, rather than putting them off until tomorrow. If God has given you a spouse, then you should love your spouse *now* instead of thinking that you will have the same opportunity tomorrow. Second, we should remember that not all of life's pleasures are appropriate for followers of God, such as the fool's laughter that Qoheleth discusses in chapter 7. The brevity of things that may seem to be pleasing should remind us that God has placed boundaries in life to enable us to live in relationship with him. Third, Qoheleth's discussion of life's brevity may come as a breath of fresh air to believers who struggle with death's long arm. We should be comforted by the promise of new life because of Christ's death and resurrection, but sometimes it is also good to acknowledge the overwhelming grief that accompanies death. Fourth, when we are confronted with difficult life events, we can trust that they also are fleeting. The good times and the bad will pass, and we can take comfort in the fact that just as things will not always be great on earth, neither will they always be terrible. In the end, we may look forward to Christ's second coming, when he will set all things right and wipe away every tear.

Discussion Questions

1. This week we spent time looking at two aspects of life that are affected profoundly by brevity: enjoyment and life itself.

Does the temporary nature of the small (and large!) pleasures in life affect the way you embrace them today? Should the brevity of life's pleasure affect the way that you live your life? What would have to change in your life if you were to live as if the things that you enjoy were not promised tomorrow? How could you use this aspect of Ecclesiastes in a ministry context?

2. The second major aspect that brevity affects is life itself. We have probably all suffered because the life of someone we love was cut short. Does it help you deal with death to know that the Bible confronts the subject head on? Does it help to know that the Bible does not sugarcoat the fact that life often ends too quickly? What are some concrete ways that you could use this aspect of Ecclesiastes to minister to those around you?

3. The other side of Qoheleth's discussion of death is that it encourages suffering people to know that their suffering will not last forever. Even if death is what brings about an end to the difficult things in life, at least they *will* end. Does this message encourage you, or is it simply morbid? In what way is it encouraging or not? Does the message change if a person is not a follower of Jesus? How can you use this aspect of Qoheleth's message to present the Gospel to a person?

4. The author of Ecclesiastes wrote the book long before Jesus came to the earth, died, and was raised again. Does Christ's death and resurrection change the message of Ecclesiastes in any way? Does Ecclesiastes's discussion of life's brevity take on a different significance when viewed through the lens of the New Testament? What changes? What remains the same?

Lesson Four

Objective: Upon completion of this lesson, you will have a clear understanding of Ecclesiastes's view of the problem of injustice in life. You will also be able to apply to your own life the lessons learned from how Ecclesiastes deals with injustice. This knowledge and application of it will enable you to cope better with unjust suffering in your life. Furthermore, the applied knowledge of Ecclesiastes's view of unjust suffering will help you to share the gospel and minister more effectively to people who have experienced unjust suffering in their lives.

Opening Prayer: Dear God, thank you for your goodness and grace, and the opportunity to study your Word more deeply. I pray that you will give me the ability to understand your Word and apply it to my life. I also pray that you will open doors for me with the people I know who are suffering and give me the opportunity to share with them the message of Ecclesiastes. May your kingdom come and your will be done on earth as it is in heaven. In Jesus's name, Amen.

Weekly Reading: Once again, this week we will read the entire book of Ecclesiastes. However, since you've been reading the book consistently for the past three weeks, you have a good understanding of the book's flow and the author's thought process. This week you will only need to read two chapters each day. Since there are only twelve chapters, this leaves you an extra day in case you have to miss a reading. You will also be reading several individual passages in the book as we work through this week's discussion of Ecclesiastes's view of injustice.

Lesson Outline:

1. The expected relationship between actions and consequences
2. The breakdown of the expected relationship between actions and consequences

Introduction

For the past three weeks we have been looking at various aspects of the book of Ecclesiastes to answer questions surrounding its authorship, time of writing, the meaning of its key word, *hebel*, and how the book views the brevity of life. During the last lesson we learned first of all that life's pleasures are fleeting, which led Qoheleth to two conclusions: first, we must not put too much stock in the foolish things of this world because they are ultimately transitory; and second, we must embrace the pleasures we are given because there is no promise that they will be here tomorrow.

We also learned that Qoheleth is deeply troubled by the fact that life itself passes too quickly. Death has troubled the human race since Adam and Eve first sinned and Abel first tasted physical death. Qoheleth's discussion of death taught us a few things. First, we can take comfort in the fact that the Bible does not tread lightly on the difficult issues that we face, such as the overpowering nature of death. Second, though Qoheleth does not talk about this, we learned that we can be comforted by the promise of the resurrection life that we will experience at Christ's second coming. Third, we learned that life's brevity can act as a comfort to those who experience intense suffering in this world. For, while their current situation is dire, they know that it will not last forever. Our lesson this week speaks to this last issue: injustice.

Qoheleth uses the term *hebel* throughout Ecclesiastes to refer to the injustice he sees around him. Specifically, the injustice Qoheleth sees results from an apparent breakdown between actions and rewards, just as we saw in the Cain and Abel narrative. At many points in Ecclesiastes Qoheleth offers consolation to those suffering injustice by stating that suffering, like the rest of life, is brief. However, there are many other times in the book when he simply laments the injustice that he witnesses. This honesty regarding the way things really are is refreshing and can perhaps go quite a long way in restoring our hope and faith in God. Before examining Qoheleth's view of injustice, we will do well to look at various passages that speak to how the world is *supposed* to work, for the world upside-down is what Qoheleth laments.

What is the Expected Relationship between Actions and Rewards?

We touched on this subject briefly in the last lesson when we talked about the fact that Abel's short life was the opposite of what was expected. As a righteous, godly person, Abel should have lived a long, full life and experienced blessing upon blessing. Instead, Abel suffered an early death that robbed him of the opportunity to experience God's blessings. This disconnect is another key aspect of Abel's life to which Qoheleth refers when he calls various situations *hebel.* The Old Testament lists several types of blessings that a godly person could expect to enjoy on earth: long life, many descendants, and provision. On the other hand, those who do not follow God can expect that their lives will be cut short and that they will be barren and destitute. Before examining the blessings and curses in the Old Testament more closely, let us look briefly at the importance of the covenant relationship with God that forms the foundation for both blessing and cursing.

Covenant Relationship in the Old Testament

Adam and Eve

The Lord formed a covenant with Adam and Eve when he placed them in the Garden that was based on Adam's and Eve's obedience to him. God gave them ample provision, a long life, and commanded them to have many children. This covenant relationship could be broken only if Adam and Eve disobeyed God by eating from the tree of the knowledge of good and evil, which they unfortunately did. As a result of their disobedience—breaking the covenant relationship—God expelled them from the Garden and placed on them a host of other consequences. What is crucial here is that the blessings Adam and Eve received resulted from God's grace—they were a *gift*—and yet their disobedience meant that the gifts were taken away. Robin Routledge puts it this way:

> This command [not to eat from the tree of the knowledge of good and evil] gave human beings an opportunity to play an active part in their relationship with God. It gave a choice: obey God's word and maintain that relationship, or disobey and reject the relationship. This shows that God wants a relationship with human beings that is entered into freely. It also emphasizes that a key element within that relationship is obedience.[1]

The Deuteronomic Covenant

Now, if we fast-forward to just after the time of Israel's exodus from Egypt we will see a similar relationship developed. God has just rescued his people from four hundred years of slavery in Egypt, delivering them through a magnificent display of his awesome power. In turn, they disobeyed by not trusting God to give them the Promised Land, which resulted in their having to wander in the wilderness for forty years. Now, they are approaching the edge of the Promised Land and are preparing to enter and conquer it. Moses, addressing the people for the final time, outlines the importance of obedience if the people are to remain in proper relationship with God, which is a prerequisite for receiving his blessings.

Just like God's covenant with Adam and Eve, the covenant the Lord makes with his people before they enter the Promised Land is grounded in God's choice of Israel. It is a gift that God gives, not something that the people can attain because of their goodness or right standing with God: "It was not because you were more

1 Robin Routledge, *Old Testament Theology: A Thematic Approach* (Downers Grove, IL: IVP Academic, 2008), 147.

in number than any other people that the Lord set his love on you and chose you, for you were the fewest of all peoples, but it is because the Lord loves you and is keeping the oath that he swore to your fathers, that the Lord has brought you out with a mighty hand and redeemed you from the house of slavery, from the hand of Pharaoh king of Egypt" (Deut 7:8–9).

In Deuteronomy, Moses traces the covenant all the way back to the relationship between the Lord and Abraham, Isaac, and Jacob (Deut 1:8). Throughout the book, Moses reminds Israel that the basis of their relationship is God's grace. However, Israel's obedience or disobedience to the Lord plays an important role both in their relationship with God and their quality of life. Deuteronomy therefore outlines the stipulations of the covenant between the Lord and Israel and the results of either keeping or failing to keep the stipulations.[1] Scholars call this aspect of the covenant retribution theology.[2] Essentially, this is the proper relationship between actions and consequences that Qoheleth expects. We saw that relationship in the disobedience of Adam and Eve, which resulted in severe consequences for the world's first humans—separation from God, difficulty in childbirth, strained relationships, and back-breaking work.

Let us first examine the results of obedience in Deuteronomy so that we may determine how Qoheleth expected the relationship between actions and rewards—retribution theology—to work. Deuteronomy 7:9–15 delineates the blessings contingent upon Israel's obedience to Yahweh:

---

1 Many scholars have pointed out similarities between Deuteronomy and Hittite Suzerainty treaties. These parallels are important for understanding the historical context of Deuteronomy as well as the pervasiveness of retributive justice in the ancient Near East. See Kenneth Kitchen, *The Bible in Its World: The Bible and Archaeology Today* (Eugene, OR: Wipf and Stock), 2004.

2 See John G. Gammie, "Theology of Retribution in the Book of Deuteronomy," *Catholic Biblical Quarterly* 32 (1970): 1–12.

> Know therefore that the LORD your God is God, the faithful God who keeps covenant and steadfast love with those who love him and keep his commandments, to a thousand generations, and repays to their face those who hate him, by destroying them. He will not be slack with one who hates him. He will repay him to his face. You shall therefore be careful to do the commandment and the statutes and the rules that I command you today.
>
> And because you listen to these rules and keep and do them, the LORD your God will keep with you the covenant and the steadfast love that he swore to your fathers. He will love you, bless you, and multiply you. He will also bless the fruit of your womb and the fruit of your ground, your grain and your wine and your oil, the increase of your herds and the young of your flock, in the land that he swore to your fathers to give you. You shall be blessed above all peoples. There shall not be male or female barren among you or among your livestock. And the LORD will take away from you all sickness, and none of the evil diseases of Egypt, which you knew, will he inflict on you, but he will lay them on all who hate you.

Importantly, the Lord once again explicitly states that the relationship between him and Israel is based solely on his covenant love towards them. There is nothing that they can *do* to earn right standing with the Lord. However, now that they are in such a covenant relationship with the Lord, they are expected to act appropriately.[1]

Deuteronomy 7 teaches that if the people obey the commands and statutes of the Lord, they will receive descendants, abundant crops and herds, and good health. The passage goes on to assure the Israelites that they will possess the land of their enemies, representing the fulfillment of God's promise to Abraham in Genesis 22. The path to these blessings is straightforward—obedience to the covenant stipulations. The context also shows that blessing comes from the Lord and is the result of his love and faithfulness to Israel's ancestors. Thus, while obedience to the covenant is paramount, it

1 Routledge, *Old Testament Theology*, 171.

is also important that the people understand that the Lord's grace is responsible for their blessing.

Deuteronomy 24:17–22 provides another clear example of the relationship between the Lord's grace and Israel's responsibility to keep the covenant stipulations:

> You shall not pervert the justice due to the sojourner or to the fatherless, or take a widow's garment in pledge, but you shall remember that you were a slave in Egypt and the LORD your God redeemed you from there; therefore I command you to do this. When you reap your harvest in your field and forget a sheaf in the field, you shall not go back to get it. It shall be for the sojourner, the fatherless, and the widow, that the LORD your God may bless you in all the work of your hands. When you beat your olive trees, you shall not go over them again. It shall be for the sojourner, the fatherless, and the widow. When you gather the grapes of your vineyard, you shall not strip it afterward. It shall be for the sojourner, the fatherless, and the widow. You shall remember that you were a slave in the land of Egypt; therefore I command you to do this.

In this passage Israel is commanded to treat the underclass in society justly and fairly. The rationale given for their treatment of the underclass is two-fold: 1) the Lord redeemed them from slavery in Egypt and 2) it enables the Lord to bless them. The author of Deuteronomy therefore shows the importance of obedience for blessing while indicating that blessing, in this case ransom from slavery, is a result of God's grace.

Deuteronomy 30:11–20 is also important for understanding the relationship between blessing and obedience in the Pentateuch:[1]

> For this commandment that I command you today is not too hard for you, neither is it far off. It is not in heaven, that you should say, "Who will ascend to heaven for us and bring it to us, that we may hear it and do it?" Neither is it beyond the sea, that you should say, "Who will go over the sea for us

1 Walter Brueggemann, "Bounded by Obedience and Praise: The Psalms as Canon," *Journal for the Study of the Old Testament* 50 (1991): 66.

> and bring it to us, that we may hear it and do it?" But the word is very near you. It is in your mouth and in your heart, so that you can do it. See, I have set before you today life and good, death and evil. If you obey the commandments of the Lord your God that I command you today, by loving the Lord your God, by walking in his ways, and by keeping his commandments and his statutes and his rules, then you shall live and multiply, and the Lord your God will bless you in the land that you are entering to take possession of it. But if your heart turns away, and you will not hear, but are drawn away to worship other gods and serve them, I declare to you today, that you shall surely perish. You shall not live long in the land that you are going over the Jordan to enter and possess. I call heaven and earth to witness against you today, that I have set before you life and death, blessing and curse. Therefore choose life, that you and your offspring may live, loving the Lord your God, obeying his voice and holding fast to him, for he is your life and length of days, that you may dwell in the land that the Lord swore to your fathers, to Abraham, to Isaac, and to Jacob, to give them.

Here Moses assures the Israelites that the commandments are doable—the commandments are near to them, in their hearts (vv. 11–14). The people therefore cannot charge the Lord with making the conditions of blessing too difficult. The passage goes on to explain what blessing consists of: descendants, reputation, physical provision—both sustenance and victory over enemies—land, and long life.

These passages in Deuteronomy show us that blessing is 1) contingent upon obedience, 2) a result of God's grace, and 3) attainable through obedience to the Lord. Now, some may raise the objection that Deuteronomy presents a covenant between the Lord and Israel that cannot be rigidly applied to individuals, in which case the book of Ecclesiastes has nothing to do with the idea of retribution theology. However, this criticism fails on two accounts. First, the commands are often individualistic in nature. Take, for example, Deuteronomy 5:21: "you shall not covet your neighbor's wife . . ." Second, the wisdom literature of the Old Testament indicates that Israel understood retribution theology to apply to individuals. Proverbs offers its readers a program of righteous living that will lead to blessing. While few scholars today would be willing to argue that Proverbs presents a rigid retribution theology, it certainly presents a worldview in which individuals are governed by the principals of retribution theology. Beyond Proverbs, the book of Job indicates that Israel applied retribution theology to individuals. Job struggles with retribution theology because, as a righteous person, he should not suffer the curses brought upon him. While the book teaches that retribution theology is not as rigid as Job's friends thought, it illustrates a common understanding of it—obedience, whether national or personal, leads to blessing and disobedience leads to curses. We will see that Ecclesiastes stands in the tradition of Job by wrestling with the inconsistencies of retribution theology.

Thus, it becomes clear from examining these passages, along with the overall trajectory of wisdom literature, that Deuteronomy presents a system of living in which people could rightly expect blessing from the Lord if they obeyed the Lord. We must stress once again that this blessing from God was the direct result of God's grace, but was contingent upon the people's obedience. Qoheleth could thus expect that obedience would result in blessings; however, what he experienced in life did not coincide with what he expected from reading Deuteronomy.

What about curses? Qoheleth expected that the wicked would receive God's judgment and was disillusioned when this did not happen. But, was he right to expect that the wicked would receive punishment? We turn again to passages in Deuteronomy to examine the idea that the unrighteous could expect punishment from God for their disobedience.

When we look at the lengthy passage of curses in Deuteronomy 28:15–68 we find the exact opposite of the blessing passages. If the people of Israel disobey the Lord, they will experience great hardship: sickness, disease, death, defeat in war, famine, barrenness, and lack of provision (unfruitful crops and the inability to eat from one's animal stock). Again, the blessing of God hinges on Israel's obedience to him and curses from God will rain down when they disobey him. The concept of retribution theology—that wrongdoing merits punishment while obedience merits reward—is carried through to its logical conclusion. Thus, we find that Qoheleth was clearly justified in his understanding of divine retribution. That he expected the obedient to be rewarded while the wicked were punished is fully in line with the theology of Deuteronomy, Proverbs, and the first parts of Genesis.

The Breakdown of the Expected Relationship between Actions and Rewards

While Qoheleth rightly expected a certain relationship between actions and rewards, he did not see that relationship playing out in everyday life. As we have seen already, the Cain and Abel narrative is the first instance in which a person's actions did not result in the expected outcome: Abel the righteous suffered the effects of the curse while Cain the wicked experienced the blessing of long life, children, and material wealth. Qoheleth therefore uses this narrative to discuss the breakdown between actions and rewards. He will eventually teach us how to interact with God in such an upside-down world, but before we reach his advice, we must work through the difficulties he sees.

Humans Cannot Really Change Anything

Qoheleth's first lament regarding the disconnect he sees comes in 1:13–15:

> And I applied my heart to seek and to search out by wisdom all that is done under heaven. It is an unhappy business that God has given to the children of man to be busy with. I have seen everything that is done under the sun, and behold, all is *hebel* and a striving after wind.
>
> What is crooked cannot be made straight,
> and what is lacking cannot be counted.

While there is some ambiguity regarding what exactly Qoheleth is talking about, the context gives us an idea: everything that is "done under heaven," a statement that Qoheleth clarifies further by noting that it is an "evil business" that God has given humans to be busy with. Thus, it seems that here Qoheleth is referring specifically to work, or the things with which humans busy themselves.[1] In what way is this *hebel*? How is this "evil" task similar to the life of Abel? Qoheleth offers readers a clue in how he qualifies his statement.

First, he is speaking specifically about things that are "done," that is, actions that humans perform. Second, Qoheleth qualifies this *hebel* statement with the words "under the sun." With this phrase Qoheleth limits his judgment to those things in the realm of humanity. Third, he parallels his *hebel* statement with the phrase "striving after wind." Most translations and commentators take the phrase as an objective genitive—"shepherding/chasing the wind."[2] However Daniel Fredericks reads the phrase as a subjective genitive, "the wind's desire," which he argues carries the connotation of "fleeting."[3] However, Qoheleth's next statement (v. 15) demonstrates that he is speaking not of the fleeting nature of wind, but of the inability of humans actually to change anything: "That which is crooked is not able to be straightened; and what is lacking is not able to be counted."[4] In this way, Qoheleth uses *hebel*, along with the guarding terms, to indicate that what humans do under the sun (and under heaven [v. 14]) does not ultimately change anything, not unlike the way in which Abel's righteous sacrifice did not change his ultimate fate—an untimely death. The issue

1 See Miller, *Symbol and Rhetoric*, 106.

2 E.g. James Bollhagen, *Ecclesiastes* (Concordia Commentary; St. Louis, MO: Concordia, 2011), 66–67; Longman, *Ecclesiastes*, 81–82.

3 Fredericks, *Ecclesiastes*, 82.

4 Author's translation.

for Qoheleth, then, is that this aspect of life is unjust—"futile and frustrating."[1]

Work Does Not Produce the Expected Results

In Ecclesiastes 2:9–11 Qoheleth picks up what is one of his favorite themes throughout the book: work. Let's read his words:

> So I became great and surpassed all who were before me in Jerusalem. Also my wisdom remained with me. And whatever my eyes desired I did not keep from them. I kept my heart from no pleasure, for my heart found pleasure in all my toil, and this was my reward for all my toil. Then I considered all that my hands had done and the toil I had expended in doing it, and behold, all was *hebel* and a striving after wind, and there was nothing to be gained under the sun.

In these few words we find that Qoheleth does indeed receive a reward for his work, namely pleasure. This is an important theme that we will pick up later, but here Qoheleth's message is clear: he expected his work to produce certain results, but those results were not forthcoming. Traditional wisdom taught that the person who worked hard would receive great benefit from his labor (for example, Prov 10:4, 14:23). Work offers a certain reward (pleasure), but the correlation between work and lasting benefit is broken. As Michael V. Fox states, ""it is not that wealth itself is trivial, but that human *efforts* are robbed of their significance by death and chance."[2]

Qoheleth continues this theme a few verses later in 2:18–26:

> I hated all my toil in which I toil under the sun, seeing that I must leave it to the man who will come after me, and who knows whether he will be wise or a fool? Yet he will be master of all for which I toiled and used my wisdom under the

1 Longman, *Ecclesiastes*, 82. Though note that Bartholomew (*Ecclesiastes*, 124) states that Qoheleth views life as an irresolvable enigma that is like attempting to chase the wind.

2 Fox, *A Time to Tear Down*, 181.

> sun. This also is *hebel.* So I turned about and gave my heart up to despair over all the toil of my labors under the sun, because sometimes a person who has toiled with wisdom and knowledge and skill must leave everything to be enjoyed by someone who did not toil for it. This also is *hebel* and a great evil. What has a man from all the toil and striving of heart with which he toils beneath the sun? For all his days are full of sorrow, and his work is a vexation. Even in the night his heart does not rest. This also is *hebel.*
>
> There is nothing better for a person than that he should eat and drink and find enjoyment in his toil. This also, I saw, is from the hand of God, for apart from him who can eat or who can have enjoyment? For to the one who pleases him God has given wisdom and knowledge and joy, but to the sinner he has given the business of gathering and collecting, only to give to one who pleases God. This also is *hebel* and a striving after wind.

Qoheleth highlights the disconnect between work, wisdom, and rewards by noting the fact that he will leave to another all that he has worked so hard and become so wise to attain.[3] Again, the referent for this *hebel* statement is injustice—the broken relationship between what one expects based on traditional wisdom theology and what one actually receives. Furthermore, Qoheleth's complaint that he does not know whether the one who inherits from him is wise or foolish may point to the fact that he does not have progeny.[4] In this case, the relationship to Abel becomes quite clear, for he also did not receive the expected blessing of children (cf. Ps 127:3–5).

After briefly discussing the injustices of death and inheritance, Qoheleth transitions back to the broken relationship between hard work and one's enjoyment of life. Longman notes that in verse 23, "Qoheleth's frustration arises out of his expectation that hard work should bring lasting reward. After all, that was what one

---

3 Thus Seow, *Ecclesiastes*, 154.

4 See also William P. Brown, *Ecclesiastes* (Interpretation; Louisville, KY: John Knox, 2000), 36.

major strand of wisdom seemed to promise."[1] Qoheleth states that humans have no real benefit from their hard work because at night they cannot rest, their work is a vexation, and their days are sorrowful. In the previous passage we looked at Qoheleth noted that pleasure in toil is a person's reward, yet here he notes even that remains elusive for some. It is no wonder, then, that he sees the *lack* of pleasure—along with the absence of other temporal pleasures such as peaceful sleep and happiness—as a bewildering breakdown between the expected relationship between work and its benefits. C. L. Seow describes it this way: "Reality contradicts the rules by which mortals conduct themselves."[2]

Furthermore, although he later expresses frustration over the righteous receiving the "rewards" of the wicked (Eccl 3:19; 8:14; 9:3), in verse 26 it seems to bother Qoheleth that even the sinner does not receive the benefit of his toil.[3] We would think Qoheleth would rejoice that God gives the work of the sinner to the "one who pleases" God; however, this also represents a breakdown in the relationship between one's actions and rewards.[4] Presumably, even the person who does not please God should be able to experience pleasure from his toil because that is his portion in this life. Qoheleth certainly argues that the wicked should receive punishment, but he likewise thinks that they should receive the benefit of their work. That they must give to another is an instance in which life is Abel-like, that is, unjust.

---

1 Longman, *Ecclesiastes,* 106.

2 Seow, *Ecclesiastes,* 156.

3 There is debate regarding whether or not the "sinner" in this passage (or the rest of wisdom literature, for that matter) carries the connotation of moral sin. See Seow, *Ecclesiastes,* 141. Against his view, see Bartholomew, *Ecclesiastes,* 151.

4 Against Bartholomew (*Ecclesiastes,* 151), who argues that Qoheleth is fully in line with traditional wisdom here in that he seeks the benefit of the righteous at the expense of the wicked.

In Ecclesiastes 4:4 Qoheleth returns to the issue of work, but this time he examines its motivations, concluding that envy motivates humanity to work.[1]

> Then I saw that all toil and all skill in work come from a man's envy of his neighbor. This also is *hebel* and a striving after wind.

According to traditional wisdom, hard work should result in riches (e.g. Prov 10:4). Not only that, but Qoheleth argues throughout his treatise that enjoyment of work itself should be motivation enough to work, for there is nothing but uncertainty regarding what will happen to the fruits of one's labor. Against this, he observes that envy for one's neighbor, rather than an appropriate expectation of return—or even the prospect of joy in work—is what truly motivates a person. The result of this observation is that Qoheleth deems this a *hebel* situation—one that is marked by injustice and the breakdown of the action-consequence of traditional wisdom. In this instance, though, the motivation behind the action—and not the consequence—is what causes him consternation.

It is also important to note that this text brings to mind Cain's jealousy of Abel by use of the term "jealousy," which in Hebrew sounds similar to Cain's name. The use of this word may be mere coincidence, or perhaps the only term for jealousy known to Qoheleth, but the preponderance of other terms and themes throughout Ecclesiastes that indicate its use of Genesis seems to demonstrate that this is at least a slight nod to the Cain and Abel narrative.

Ecclesiastes 4:13–16 presents us with a brief story of the rise of a king that has caused no small amount of confusion among interpreters through the years. The text reads:

> Better was a poor and wise youth than an old and foolish king who no longer knew how to take advice. For he went from prison to the throne, though in his own kingdom he had been born poor. I saw all the living who move about under

---

1 Cf. Fox, *A Time to Tear Down and a Time to Build Up*, 220.

> the sun, along with that youth who was to stand in the king's place. There was no end of all the people, all of whom he led. Yet those who come later will not rejoice in him. Surely this also is *hebel* and a striving after wind.

That a poor, wise youth went from prison to the throne is not problematic for Qoheleth. In fact, Qoheleth would have applauded the elevation of a person based on his wisdom. It is unclear to whom this text refers, or if it refers to an actual person at all. Douglas Miller tentatively suggests that this text may call to mind Joseph's rise to power in Egypt.[1] But, Qoheleth could just as easily be using a well-known story to demonstrate his larger point. Whomever Qoheleth has in mind, it is clear that he is lamenting the fact that the young man is quickly forgotten by those who come after him and that they do not rejoice in him. This section also calls to mind Qoheleth's earlier *hebel* statement in which he laments the uncertainty of the quality of person who will come after him (Eccl 2:19). A good, wise king should presumably be remembered by those who come after him, yet no such thing happens in this case. The expected consequence of effective, wise ruling—remembrance—is absent in this case, and leads Qoheleth to declare that this is *hebel.*

Qoheleth brings up the issue of injustice once again in 6:1–6:

> There is an evil that I have seen under the sun, and it lies heavy on mankind: a man to whom God gives wealth, possessions, and honor, so that he lacks nothing of all that he desires, yet God does not give him power to enjoy them, but a stranger enjoys them. This is *hebel*; it is a grievous evil. If a man fathers a hundred children and lives many years, so that the days of his years are many, but his soul is not satisfied with life's good

1 Douglas Miller, "Power in Wisdom: The Suffering Servant of Ecclesiastes 4," in *Peace and Justice Shall Embrace: Power and Theopolitics in the Bible, Essays in Honor of Millard Lind* (ed. Ted Grimsrud and Loren Johns; Telford, PA: Pandora, 1999), 145–73.

> things, and he also has no burial, I say that a stillborn child is better off than he. For it comes in *hebel* and goes in darkness, and in darkness its name is covered. Moreover, it has not seen the sun or known anything, yet it finds rest rather than he. Even though he should live a thousand years twice over, yet enjoy no good—do not all go to the one place?

Here Qoheleth argues that when a person is given gifts by God, such as wealth, children, and long life, but is unable to enjoy those things, *hebel* abounds. Should not the person to whom God gives good things be able to enjoy them? The subject in mind is therefore not so much the good things in life, but a person's inability to enjoy them. Qoheleth highly values God's sovereignty in this instance, noting that both the ability to enjoy and the things to be enjoyed come from God. Qoheleth notes that this inability to enjoy is inherently evil and unjust because a person *should* be able to enjoy God's gifts; however, such enjoyment is entirely out of human control, signifying again the disconnect between actions and rewards.

Ecclesiastes 7:15 expands the discussion of the breakdown between actions and rewards by turning to the fate of the righteous and the wicked:

> In my *hebel* life I have seen everything. There is a righteous man who perishes in his righteousness, and there is a wicked man who prolongs his life in his evildoing.

We mentioned earlier that this passage deals with one of the primary issues for Qoheleth—the overwhelming nature of death itself. And yet there is another aspect that weighs upon Qoheleth: the fact that the righteous person perishes while the wicked person lives a long life. It is highly discomforting to Qoheleth that the wise person would die an untimely death because the traditional theology to which he holds teaches that the wise would live long, not unlike the patriarchs we see in the Old Testament.[1] Not only does Qoheleth see precedence for long life in the righteous lives of the

1 Bartholomew, *Ecclesiastes*, 255.

patriarchs, but we also saw that Deuteronomy teaches that long life is the reward of those who follow God. Such breakdown between expectations and reality cause Qoheleth no little frustration.

In Ecclesiastes 8:10–15 we find our final statements from Qoheleth regarding the injustices he sees in life:

> Then I saw the wicked buried. They used to go in and out of the holy place and were praised in the city where they had done such things. This also is *hebel.* Because the sentence against an evil deed is not executed speedily, the heart of the children of man is fully set to do evil. Though a sinner does evil a hundred times and prolongs his life, yet I know that it will be well with those who fear God, because they fear before him. But it will not be well with the wicked, neither will he prolong his days like a shadow, because he does not fear before God. There is a *hebel* that takes place on earth, that there are righteous people to whom it happens according to the deeds of the wicked, and there are wicked people to whom it happens according to the deeds of the righteous. I said that this also is *hebel.* And I commend joy, for man has nothing better under the sun but to eat and drink and be joyful, for this will go with him in his toil through the days of his life that God has given him under the sun.

Qoheleth presents several important concepts in this text. First, we note that he describes three aspects of life that should be reserved for the righteous: a proper burial, access to God, and the reception of praise. However, instead of these honors being reserved for the righteous only, Qoheleth notes that the *wicked* receive these good things, which simply should not be. Not only that, but the wicked person is allowed to continue sinning with no ramifications. How many times have we seen similar situations, in which we cried out to God because the wicked go on sinning with no real punishment for their sin? Qoheleth rightly notes that foolish people will take this lack of punishment as an encouragement to continue in their sinful ways. He then goes on to describe a situation in verse 14 in which the righteous person receives the reward of the wicked, which only heightens his frustration that the wicked receive the reward of the righteous. We again see in these verses an echo of Abel's life, who was the first person to suffer the fate of the wicked.

The second important aspect of these verses is that Qoheleth assures his readers that the wicked person will not always experience good things. Indeed, God *will* judge the sinner for his sins and welcome the righteous person into his kingdom. Here it seems that Qoheleth hints at an important concept that the New Testament fully develops. Although life may seem unjust here and now—where believers in Christ are persecuted while evil people revel in wealth and luxury—there is a final judgment coming in which Jesus will set all things right and welcome the faithful into his kingdom. Qoheleth therefore offers a glimpse of the hope that we have in God, a hope that will not be disappointed even though our current situation may seem otherwise.

Finally, the third noteworthy aspect of this passage is that Qoheleth commends joy in the face of the unjust exaltation of the wicked. Qoheleth rightly understands that we humans can do very little to effect any real change in life. In light of our weakness, he commends the enjoyment of that which God has given us the ability to enjoy. However, we would be wrong to think that Qoheleth is commending the type of hedonistic pleasure that throws all caution to the wind. We know from his statement regarding God's ultimate judgment that he is not encouraging believers to engage in wanton sin. Nevertheless, we would be equally remiss if we were to think that enjoyment of God's gifts indicates sinfulness. As Dietrich Bonhoeffer states,

> I believe that we ought to love and trust God in our *lives*, and in all the good things he sends us, that when the time comes (but not before!) we may go to him with love, trust, and joy. But, to put it plainly, for a man in his wife's arms to be hankering after the other world is, in mild terms, a piece of bad taste, and not God's will. We ought to find and love God in what he actually gives us; if it pleases him to allow us to enjoy some overwhelming earthly happiness, we must not

try to be more pious than God himself and allow our earthly happiness to be corrupted by presumption and arrogance, and by unbridled religious fantasy which is never satisfied with what God gives. God will see to it that the man who finds in him his earthly happiness and thanks him for it does not lack reminder that earthly things are transient, that it is good for him to attune his heart to what is eternal, and that sooner or later there will be times when he can say in all sincerity, "I wish I were home." But everything has its time, and the main thing is that we keep step with God, and do not keep pressing on a few steps ahead—nor keep dawdling a step behind. It's presumptuous to want to have everything at once—matrimonial bliss, the cross, and the heavenly Jerusalem, where they neither marry nor are given in marriage. "For everything there is a season" (Eccles. 3.1); everything has its time: "a time to weep, and a time to laugh; . . . a time to embrace, and a time to refrain from embracing; . . . a time to rend, and a time to sew . . . and God seeks again what is past."[1]

Discussion Questions

1. This week we spent our time looking at one of the most perplexing issues that we face in the Christian life: the apparent breakdown between actions and their consequences. Certainly we have all experienced situations that we found painfully unjust, situations where wicked people prospered while godly people suffered. In the past, how have you dealt with the frustration that such situations cause? How have you been able to maintain your faith in a just and righteous God when you see the wicked prosper?

2. After reading through all of these passaes in which Qoheleth discusses very depressing subjects again and again,

1 Dietrich Bonhoeffer, *Letters and Papers from Prison* (trans. Reginald H. Fuller and Frank Clarke; ed. Eberhard Bethge; New York: Macmillan, 1972), 168–69. Quoted in James Limburg, *Encountering Ecclesiastes: A Book for Our Time* (Grand Rapids, MI: Eerdmans, 2006), 50–51.

why do you think this book is in the Bible? How is this book applicable to faith and life today? Does it contradict other parts of Scripture?

3. How does the New Testament deal with injustice and suffering? What difference does the cross of Christ make when we are discussing this issue?

4. Why do you think the principle of retribution exists in the Bible? How (if at all) is it changed by the New Testament? How does it apply to our lives today?

Lesson Five

Objective: Upon completion of this lesson, you will have a clear understanding of how Ecclesiastes suggests that we cope with the frustrations and injustices that life brings. This understanding will allow you to put the previous two lessons, which dealt with death and the injustice Qoheleth sees in life, into its appropriate context. You should be able to apply this knowledge to your own life so that you are better equipped to deal with life's difficulties from a biblical standpoint. This knowledge will also strengthen your faith and trust in God by showing how you can enjoy his gifts, even in the midst of an uncertain world, which will in turn equip you to share the gospel with and minister to those who find themselves doubting God because of the unjust suffering they see around them.

Opening Prayer: Dear God, thank you for your goodness and grace, and the opportunity to study your Word more deeply. I pray that you will give me the ability to understand the message of Ecclesiastes and to apply it to my life in a way that glorifies you. Please also give me the opportunity to enjoy the gifts that you have given and protect me from the bitterness that so often comes along with unjust suffering. I pray that as I internalize the truth from your Word that you will give me the opportunity to minister to those who also need to hear it. May your kingdom come and your will be done on earth as it is in heaven. In Jesus's name, Amen

Weekly Reading: Once again, this week we will read the entire book of Ecclesiastes. However, since you've been reading the book consistently for the past four weeks, you have a good understanding of the book's flow and the author's thought process. This week you will only need to read two chapters each day. Since there are only twelve chapters, this leaves you an extra day in case you have to miss a reading. You will also be reading several individual passages in the book as we work through this week's discussion of Ecclesiastes's view of injustice.

Lesson Outline:

1. Despite death and injustice, enjoy!
2. Enjoyment in the Christian life today

Introduction

The book of Ecclesiastes has much to say about how we are supposed to get along in this world full of death and injustice. In a nutshell, Qoheleth encourages his readers—and us today—to take joy in God's gifts. We saw earlier that God's gifts, just like life itself, are fleeting. However, this very quality should propel us to enjoy them even further. To that end, we find throughout Ecclesiastes several statements in which Qoheleth calls his readers to take joy in various aspects of life if and when God allows it. Craig Bartholomew has noted that these so-called *carpe diem* ("seize the day") passages represent a return to humanity's pre-fall condition, where Adam and Eve enjoyed perfect relationship with God and each other before their (and our) lives were tarnished by the ugly stain of sin.[1]

In this lesson we will work through each of the "enjoy" passages in Ecclesiastes in order to examine how Qoheleth frames his discussion on joy so that we may learn what our response should be in light of death's eventuality and the presence of injustice and uncertainty in life. In the next lesson we will examine the overall message of Ecclesiastes, paying special attention to the importance that it places on fearful obedience to God. That discussion will help us to place Qoheleth's call to enjoyment in its appropriate context. But first we turn to the passages in which Qoheleth sets out his program for coping with a world turned upside-down.

1 Bartholomew, *Ecclesiastes*, 150–53.

Despite Death and Injustice, Enjoy!

Ecclesiastes 2:24–26

> There is nothing better for a person than that he should eat and drink and find enjoyment in his toil. This also, I saw, is from the hand of God, for apart from him who can eat or who can have enjoyment? For to the one who pleases him God has given wisdom and knowledge and joy, but to the sinner he has given the business of gathering and collecting, only to give to one who pleases God. This also is *hebel* and a striving after wind.

We find Qoheleth's first call to enjoyment in chapter two, just after he discusses the injustices he sees in that the wise and foolish alike are forgotten when they die (2:12–17), and that he works hard only to leave his profits to an unknown person who will come after him (2:18–23). There are several important aspects to Qoheleth's call to enjoyment that will help us to understand how to apply it to life today.

First, Qoheleth here looks back to the pleasures that humans experienced before the fall. As we pointed out in lesson two, this passage draws on thematic elements from the narrative of the Garden of Eden in the early chapters of Genesis. When God placed humans in the Garden of Eden he gave them free reign to eat from any fruit in the entire garden (including the tree of life), save the fruit from the tree of the knowledge of good and evil (Gen 2:17). This freedom indicates that God intended the humans to *enjoy* the fruits of the garden—food was not to be some sort of hidden pleasure, but rather a gift freely enjoyed by those in proper relationship with him. That Qoheleth encourages readers to enjoy their food points back to this time before the fall when God's people could eat freely from the fruit of the garden, a time before we had to produce our food by the sweat of our brow.

Also important is the fact that Qoheleth encourages enjoyment from toil, which likewise points back to a time before work included hard labor that produced meager results. When God placed Adam in the Garden of Eden his intent was for Adam to "work it and keep it" (Gen 2:15). After Adam and Eve break their covenant relationship with God by eating from the tree of the knowledge of good and evil, God curses the ground so that work will become toilsome for Adam:

> Because you have listened to the voice of your wife and have eaten of the tree of which I commanded you, "You shall not eat of it," cursed is the ground because of you; in pain you shall eat of it all the days of your life; thorns and thistles it shall bring forth for you; and you shall eat the plants of the field. By the sweat of your face you shall eat bread, till you return to the ground, for out if it you were taken; for you are dust, and to dust you shall return. (Gen 3:17–19)

The combination of these two passages, with God first blessing Adam's work and then cursing it, indicates that work was initially meant to be a joyful, fulfilling experience. Thus, as Bartholomew indicates, Qoheleth here envisions a return to the pre-fall life experienced in the Garden of Eden, when work was a pleasurable experience that fproduced the expected results.[1]

The second important aspect of this text is its emphasis on God's sovereignty. Qoheleth states in no uncertain terms that "This also, I saw, is from the hand of God, for apart from him who can eat or who can have enjoyment?" All enjoyment of work, eating, and drinking comes directly from the hand of God. It is he who allows humans to enjoy life, and it is he who controls every facet of our lives. As believers in the Western world we would do well to remember this very thing, for so often it is easy to attribute the good things in life—a job we love, the food we eat, the clothes we wear—to our own ingenuity, hard work, or even good luck. However, Qoheleth, like James, reminds us that "Every good and every perfect gift is from above, coming down from the Father of lights with whom there is no variation or shadow due to change" (James 1:17). Bartholomew points out that an important implica-

1 See Bartholomew, *Ecclesiastes*, 151–2.

tion of Qoheleth's statements about food is that Christians should be aware of the food we eat and recognize that it is God's gift to us.[1] Rather than greedy over-consumption of food (along with other goods), we should give thanks to God and remember that it is he who has allowed us the pleasure of eating. This acknowledgement will enable us to give more freely to others who may not have the same access to one of life's pleasures—food—because it reminds that what he have received is also a gift.

Related to the fact that God is the giver of all gifts is Qoheleth's recognition that God gives good things to those who obey him. While we noted previously that Qoheleth seems disconcerted that the fruits of a person's labor—in this case, the one who displeases God—do not always match his efforts, it nevertheless remains that God is free to give to those who please him (as well as to those who do not please him: "For he makes his sun rise on the evil and the good, and sends rain on the just and on the unjust" [Matt 5:45]). Rather than being an encouragement to sin willfully with the assumption that God will bless us no matter what, this statement in Ecclesiastes should encourage us to follow closely after God and to walk in obedience to him. We do not serve God because he may or may not bless us, but because he is himself God, the sovereign Ruler of all life. Furthermore, we must realize that while God does bless those who obey him, blessing may not always come during this life—a fact that causes Qoheleth consternation. Therefore, while it is encouraging to know that God blesses those who obey him, we must also remember that this blessing may come in the next life, for—as Jesus's example demonstrates—obedience to God may mean death.

In sum, the important aspects of this passage for our study today are that Qoheleth encourages us to return to a place before the fall, a place where people enjoyed God's gift of food without sinning and were able to take great joy in their God-given vocations. Thanks to the salvific death of Christ, we may now do just that. Also key for believers today is the recognition that God is the

1 Ibid., 154–55.

sovereign Giver of all good gifts. We can enjoy nothing apart from him. And yet, it is also critical to realize that enjoyment of God's gifts is a positive aspect of life on earth. As Bonhoeffer stated, if God has given us the opportunity to enjoy, then we would do well to take hold of that opportunity with a thankful heart.

Ecclesiastes 3:10–15

> I have seen the business that God has given to the children of man to be busy with. He has made everything beautiful in its time. Also, he has put eternity into man's heart, yet so that he cannot find out what God has done from the beginning to the end. I perceived that there is nothing better for them than to be joyful and to do good as long as they live; also that everyone should eat and drink and take pleasure in all his toil—this is God's gift to man. I perceived that whatever God does endures forever; nothing can be added to it, nor anything taken from it. God has done it, so that people fear before him. That which is, already has been; that which is to be, already has been; and God seeks what has been driven away.

This next call to joy comes just after Qoheleth explores the proper times for certain activities. In his final estimation, there is an appropriate time for all things: God has "made everything beautiful in its time." Not only that, but God "has placed eternity into man's heart" and yet still hides from humans his plans and actions. Walter Kaiser notes that the idea of God's placing eternity in the human heart points to "a deep-seated desire, a compulsive drive . . . to know the character, composition, and meaning of the world . . . and to discern its purpose and destiny."[1] This desire to seek out the eternity he has put in our hearts is part of what God has orchestrated in humans so that we will seek to know and love him. However, Qoheleth also states clearly that humanity cannot know what God is doing. Thus, since humans cannot know what

---

1 Walter C. Kaiser, Jr. *Ecclesiastes: Total Life* (Everyman's Bible Commentary; Chicago: Moody, 1979). Quoted in Longman, *Ecclesiastes*, 121.

it is that God is about, and since it is God who has set the appropriate time for all things, the role of humans is simply to take joy, do good, and enjoy the fleeting pleasure of life such as food, drink, and work. We can make similar comments regarding this passage as the previous one.

First, it is important to note that Qoheleth highlights God's sovereignty with his statements regarding the fact that God makes everything beautiful, that God gives people tasks to do, that God's actions endure forever, and that the appropriate human response is fear of God. Given God's sovereign nature, it is as critical for believers today as it was for believers when Ecclesiastes was first written to submit themselves to his authority. The appropriate response to a sovereign God is not sinfulness, but rather fear of God, which exhibits itself in obedience to him.

Second, we see once again that the things Qoheleth encourages—enjoyment in work, food, and drink—are the very things that Adam and Eve enjoyed in their pre-fall state in the Garden of Eden. Furthermore, God makes all of these things beautiful in their own time. Daniel Fredericks remarks that this "is the greatest statement of divine providence in the whole of Scripture. It is the theorem from which the believer's hope is derived that all things work together for good for those who love God (Rom. 8:28)."[1] Because God is always working things out in their own time, the believer can hope in God, trust in his providence and provision, and enjoy those things that God has given him or her to enjoy. Fredericks goes on to note that the issue of timing is crucial in this passage, for God makes everything beautiful in its time (or *his* time, according to the way one translates the Hebrew pronoun). It is up to the follower of God to discern the proper time for actions, "just as God does."[2] This is where wisdom comes into play, for the believer should seek God constantly and use sound judgment concerning when the time is "beautiful" for particular actions.

---

1 Fredericks, *Ecclesiastes*, 117.

2 Ibid., 118.

Third, Qoheleth brings up the issue of doing "good" in this passage, which he did not mention in the previous statement regarding joy. Here he notes in no uncertain terms that it is important for people to pursue "moral uprightness."[1] Although some scholars argue that this verse does not carry the moral sense of the word—that is, "doing good"—the immediate context, with its admonition to fear God, as well as the context of the entire book, would suggest that Qoheleth is indeed talking about the importance of pursuing righteousness, rather than simply the enjoyment of life.[2]

Thus, we find in this passage primarily the same concerns we found in Ecclesiastes 2:24–26, though approached from a slightly different direction. Here Qoheleth explores the issues of time and appropriateness, as well as God's placing eternity in the human heart. The result of human inability to know what God is up to is that they should trust and fear him, and enjoy his gifts, such as working, eating, and drinking. However, Qoheleth adds to this that humans should also seek to do good in God's sight. As we move forward in our lesson, and especially in the final lesson, we will see ever more clearly the high value that Qoheleth places on obedience to God, that is, on "doing good." We turn now to the next set of verses in which Qoheleth offers advice for those walking about in this mysterious world of injustice.

Ecclesiastes 3:16–22

> Moreover, I saw under the sun that in the place of justice, even there was wickedness, and in the place of righteousness, even there was wickedness. I said in my heart, God will judge the righteous and the wicked, for there is a time for every matter and for every work. I said in my heart with regard to the children of man that God is testing them that they may see that they themselves are but beasts. For what happens to the children of man and what happens to the beasts is the same; as

---

1 Ibid.

2 See Tremper Longman, *Ecclesiastes*, 122.

> one dies, so dies the other. They all have the same breath, and man has no advantage over the beasts, for all is *hebel.* All go to one place. All are from the dust, and to dust all return. Who knows whether the spirit of man goes upward and the spirit of the beast goes down into the earth? So I saw that there is nothing better than that a man should rejoice in his work, for that is his lot. Who can bring him to see what will be after him?

Building on his statements in 3:10–15, Qoheleth returns to the theme of enjoyment in life after exploring another perplexing issue that we examined closely in lesson three: the inescapability of death. At this juncture Qoheleth offers the same advice we find throughout the book: in light of the fact that humans and animals suffer the same fate, humans should rejoice in work. This advice speaks clearly to Qoheleth's concern that we as humans do not worry about the things over which we have no control, such as death. Rather than fretting over the inevitable, humans should rejoice in their work, which is something that they *can* do, if God allows them that pleasure.

It is also important to note that this passage echoes a familiar refrain from Proverbs: that hard work has its own rewards. We know from elsewhere in Ecclesiastes that hard work does not always result in enjoyment of the fruits of that work; nevertheless, Qoheleth advises that we act wisely by working hard and enjoying the work we do. Thus, while he is cognizant that life does not always go as planned, he does not completely eschew traditional wisdom. We would do well to follow his advice today and enjoy our work if God has so allowed it.

Qoheleth ends this discussion of death and enjoyment by asking the rhetorical question, "Who can bring him to see what will be after him?" Of course, we know the answer to that question is God himself can allow us to see what will come after us, and in a very real sense he has allowed New Testament believers a glimpse into the eschatological future. We know from Revelation 20 that there will be a great judgment at the end of days, in which all things are set right and the people of God are welcomed into his rest while those who rebel against God are sent into eternal judgment.[1] Believers today can therefore take great comfort through the revelation of the New Testament. We know emphatically that we will one day be with Christ in perfected bodies. Such knowledge should drive us to obey, honor, and serve him. However, even without that knowledge, we should stand with the Old Testament saints in our faithful obedience to God. According to Ecclesiastes, part of that obedience entails taking enjoyment in the pleasures that God has given. Thus, while here on this earth, we should work diligently and take pleasure in the vocation God has given us.

Ecclesiastes 5:18–20

> Behold, what I have seen to be good and fitting is to eat and drink and find enjoyment in all the toil with which one toils under the sun the few days of his life that God has given him, for this is his lot. Everyone also to whom God has given wealth and possessions and power to enjoy them, and to accept his lot and rejoice in his toil—this is the gift of God. For he will not much remember the days of his life because God keeps him occupied with joy in his heart.

Qoheleth returns to this encouragement to enjoy life after walking his readers through a thoroughly depressing and unjust situation: the person who amasses a great amount of wealth, but loses it all before he can enjoy it. Qoheleth reminds us that we will leave this earth just as we entered it, with nothing at all. Qoheleth does not leave us with only a stark reminder of death's finality; instead, he shows us the proper way to live life. Whenever God allows us some gift, it is "good and fitting" to enjoy it, whether it be food and drink, our work, or our possessions. We must grasp hold of these things and enjoy them in the moment because, as the story Qoheleth relates in 5:13–17 indicates, we will not be taking those things with us into death.

---

1 Bartholomew, *Ecclesiastes*, 179.

One of the most important concepts to consider in this text is that Qoheleth does not specify enjoyment solely for those who are rich. God certainly gives differing amounts of wealth and possessions to each person, but we should remember that these things are just that—gifts. Thus, we should strive to enjoy whatever gifts God has given. Rather than being like the ungrateful servants in Matthew 20, we should strive for a thankful heart that embraces all that God gives us, no matter what he chooses to give our neighbor.

When read in conjunction with the previous passage regarding the man who keeps wealth to his own detriment, this text becomes a shocking wake-up call to many of us in the West, most especially in the United States. Americans, Christians included, are well-known for our opulent wealth and constant desire for more. I do not intend to argue that all wealth is bad, for as Qoheleth teaches, God is the one who gives and takes away. Far be it from Christians to scorn the things God has given. Yet, we must temper our understanding of God's gift of wealth with the warning that it will do us no good if kept to ourselves. Furthermore, amassing more and more—just to have it—is a dangerous road to travel, as we learn both from Ecclesiastes and Jesus himself (e.g. Matt 6:19–24; 19:16–30). Therefore, wealthy Christians (and most all Americans are wealthy by global standards) must think long and hard about how we use our wealth.

Another aspect of this text worth pondering is what Qoheleth means when he states that the joy given by God will occupy his heart so that he will "not remember much the days of his life." Such a statement sounds strange coming from Qoheleth because elsewhere he encourages reflection on death, going so far as to say that "the heart of the wise is in the house of mourning" (Eccl 7:4). Furthermore, Qoheleth also encourages reflection on life, which is essentially what his entire treatise is—a discussion of the injustices faced by humans during life "under the sun." And yet here he seems to imply that it is *good* not to remember these sorts of things, the evil things that happen to people in life. However, Qoheleth's observation about the benefit of being preoccupied with enjoyment—not remembering the bad days—is in keeping with his overall admonition to enjoy God's gifts while trusting in his sovereignty to care for everything else. Bollhagen states it this way:

> Regarding the present with all its problems, God induces an amnesia of another sort: he keeps people so busy that they have no time to worry or get depressed about life in general. As God takes care of the bigger, overarching problems of life, he gives all people little problems and challenges that monopolize their time day by day. In other words, every person in the world has to let God perform his business out of sheer personal necessity.[1]

Bollhagen goes on to state that the "situation is further enhanced in the life of the trusting child of God. His preoccupation is mingled with joy of heart . . . He knows that his God—omnipotent, wise, and gracious—is equal to the task. He also knows that God is doing the job, that God does make everything work together for good (Rom 8:28) . . ."[2]

In sum, Qoheleth encourages followers of God to hold these two things in tension: thoughtful reflection on life's realities and trust in the goodness and sovereignty of God while enjoying his gifts. Engaging in each of these practices is wise behavior, so we should not shy away from holding them in tension with each other. Rather than being a contradictory either/or situation, this is a complementary both/and situation. Wisdom entails doing each at the appropriate time.

Ecclesiastes 8:10–15

> Then I saw the wicked buried. They used to go in and out of the holy place and were praised in the city where they had done such things. This also is *hebel.* Because the sentence against an evil deed is not executed speedily, the heart of the children of man is fully set to do evil. Though a sinner does

1 Bollhagen, *Ecclesiastes*, 212.

2 Ibid.

> evil a hundred times and prolongs his life, yet I know that it will be well with those who fear God, because they fear before him. But it will not be well with the wicked, neither will he prolong his days like a shadow, because he does not fear before God. There is a *hebel* that takes place on earth, that there are righteous people to whom it happens according to the deeds of the wicked, and there are wicked people to whom it happens according to the deeds of the righteous. I said that this also is *hebel*. And I commend joy, for man has no good thing under the sun but to eat and drink and be joyful, for this will go with him in his toil through the days of his life that God has given him under the sun.

We have already discussed this passage in our treatment of the meaning of *hebel* and the role that injustice plays in Ecclesiastes as a whole. We turn to it here because of the advice Qoheleth gives in light of the injustice of the prosperity of the wicked. He first comforts the reader with the statement that the wicked really will be punished, even though it appears that in this life wicked people often prosper for far longer than is just. Qoheleth does not stop at that, though, as he next offers a piece of advice for those who see such injustices in the world: take joy in the things that can be enjoyed, such as eating and drinking.

Daniel Fredericks is right to point out that Qoheleth's commendation of joy in verse 15 is "a commendable way of life on its own merits, even before the Fall. Finding happiness in our responsible daily work is the intent of the Hebr[ew] here rather than interpretations that render this refrain in shallow and frivolous terms, like 'having fun' (NLT)."[1] Thus, we should be careful not to denigrate the meaning of this passage into a hedonistic statement that encourages over-indulgence in sinful activity. Remember Qoheleth's previous statement, in which he spoke of the importance of fearing God. This statement is an encouragement to return to the pre-fall life in which humans enjoyed perfect relationship with their Creator and went about eating, drinking, working, and en-

1 Fredericks, *Ecclesiastes*, 198.

joying each other's companionship. In the same way, to the person who experiences unjust suffering in this life, Qoheleth encourages a return to a life full of enjoyment of God's gifts.

This enjoyment also contains the important element of trusting in God. God has given the gifts of work, food, and enjoyment of each of these things. By taking the opportunity simply to enjoy these gifts, the believer today indicates an implicit trust in the good nature of our sovereign God. Rather than worrying about "your life, what you will eat, or what you will drink" (Matt 6:25), the person who trusts in God to provide these things is free to *enjoy* them. As Qoheleth states, such joy in life "will go with him in his toil through the days of his life that God has given him under the sun."

Therefore, this passage reminds us of three important issues for life today. First, life ultimately will not go well for those who disobey God. Even though this may seem to be the case in the present, we can trust that those who fear God are the true winners, both in this life and the next. This is because in this life they can rest in the blessed assurance that God is sovereign and they are free to enjoy the gifts he gives; in the next life they will have perfect communion with him. While this latter concept is not explicit in Ecclesiastes, believers on this side of the cross know that the death and resurrection of Christ has made this possible. Second, by taking joy in God's good gifts instead of fretting over things outside of our control, we are acknowledging the lordship of Christ and trusting in his ability and promise to provide for our needs. Third, we can have certainty that all of the good things in life come from none other than God himself, who will "give good things to those who ask him" (Matt 7:11).

Ecclesiastes 9:7–10

> Go, eat your bread with joy, and drink your wine with a merry heart, for God has already approved what you do. Let your garments be always white. Let not oil be lacking on your

> head. Enjoy life with the wife whom you love, all the days of your *hebel* life that he has given you under the sun, because that is your portion in life and in your toil at which you toil under the sun. Whatever your hand finds to do, do it with your might, for there is no work or thought or knowledge or wisdom in Sheol, to which you are going.

Qoheleth's next statement of joy once again comes on the heels of a discussion about the inevitability of death. Bartholomew states that Qoheleth does not offer his advice as an "answer to the enigma of death, but [as] an alternative vision of life."[1] Bartholomew is absolutely correct about these *carpe diem* passages presenting a different way to live life, a way that hearkens back to the Garden of Eden. However, this is not necessarily an either/or situation. Given the context of this passage, as well as the other *carpe diem* passages—set against the backdrop of some unjust or frustrating situation—it is likely that Qoheleth presents *both* an alternative way to live life *and* an answer to death's overpowering inevitability.

In this section Fredericks rightly points out that Qoheleth offers "refreshing elaborations on what was becoming formulaic."[2] That is, the readers have by this point begun to expect that Qoheleth is going to make some sort of comment about how taking joy in God's gifts is better than this thing or that thing. Instead, we are confronted with a series of images that commend us in no uncertain terms to take great joy in the gifts that God has given in this life. Qoheleth speaks about having a merry heart, enjoying one's wife (which of course can be applied to a wife enjoying her husband), having white garments, and never lacking oil on one's head. Some of these images translate well into the modern Western context, but not so much others. Who puts oil on their heads nowadays? And who always wears white? Is there not some rule forbidding this after Labor Day?

Interpreters are divided regarding the meaning of "white" in this context, but the most likely candidate for the proper in-

---

1 Bartholomew, *Ecclesiastes*, 303.

2 Fredericks, *Ecclesiastes*, 208.

terpretation seems to be "purity, festiveness, or elevated status."[1] Bartholomew argues that the purity reflected by white should also be combined with a note of hope because of the context of the passage.[2] Oil likewise is a common element associated with joy (see, for example, Ps 23:5). A brief comparison with other ancient Near Eastern literature indicates that this interpretation is on the mark. For example, the *Epic of Gilgamesh* states,

> Of each day make thou a feast of rejoicing,
> Day and night dance thou and play!
> Let thy garments be sparkling fresh,
> Thy head be washed; bathe thou in water.
> Pay heed to the little one that holds onto thy hand
> Let thy spouse delight in thy bosom! . . .
> Put myrrh upon thy head and clothing of fine linen.[3]

This passage demonstrates that the images of white (i.e. "fresh") garments and oil upon one's head were clear indicators of joy. Thus, to bring this to the modern context, Qoheleth is stating that people should wear clean, fresh clothes and perfume, "dress up" as it were. Their outward appearance should match the inward state of their hearts: joy.

Some commentators argue that the "wife" in this passage is not necessarily a person's wife, but simply a "woman" that a man loves. However, as Bartholomew points out, the context indicates that this word does indeed refer to a wife, as it is rooted in "a theology of creation" in which God created a particular man and a particular woman who were married to each other: "Thus v. 9a is a positive affirmation of marriage that is to be fully enjoyed in all

---

1 A. Brenner, *Colour Terms in the Old Testament* (JSOT Supplement 21; Sheffield: JSOT Press, 1982), 152. Cited in Bartholomew, *Ecclesiastes*, 304.

2 Bartholomew, 304.

3 *Epic of Gilgamesh*, in *Ancient Near Eastern Texts Relating to the Old Testament* (3rd ed.; ed. J. B. Pritchard; Princeton: Princeton University Press, 1969), 467. Quoted in Fredericks, *Ecclesiastes*, 209.

its dimensions."[1] This statement regarding the bliss of marriage as it relates to living life in proper relationship to God and others is an important reminder to our culture today, which increasingly devalues marriage. Marriage is a God-ordained relationship that, when lived out properly, leads to great joy in the relationship and an outstanding witness for Christ. Rather than seeking "love" in a series of relationships outside of marriage, the person who would find and keep true joy should seek fulfillment with his or her spouse.

Finally, Qoheleth once again commends joy in work. However, he expands his statements about work to include working "with your might." The person who would follow the Lord must find joy in *hard* work, not simply work. It is not enough to go about one's work half-heartedly. This work ethic is reinforced when we come to the New Testament, where we are also encouraged to work hard, "as for the Lord and not for men" (Col 3:23; cf. 2 Thess 3:10–12).

Ecclesiastes 11:7–10

> Light is sweet, and it is pleasant for the eyes to see the sun. So if a person lives many years, let him rejoice in them all; but let him remember that the days of darkness will be many. All that comes is *hebel*. Rejoice, O young man, in your youth, and let your heart cheer you in the days of your youth. Walk in the ways of your heart and the sight of your eyes. But know that for all these things God will bring you into judgment. Remove vexation from your heart, and put away pain from your body, for youth and the dawn of life are *hebel*.

In this final *carpe diem* passage Qoheleth reminds his readers once again that they should rejoice when the opportunity arises. Specifically, one should rejoice in all of his years, but especially when one is young because "youth and the dawn of life are *hebel*" (that is, fleeting). Qoheleth's statement in verse 7 reminds us that one of life's simple pleasures—to see the sun—should not be taken for granted. Most people can relate to the joy that comes on that

1 Bartholomew, *Ecclesiastes*, 305.

first day of spring, when the clouds finally break and the sun shines through to warm us. It is one of the small gifts that God has allowed humans to enjoy, and one that we should not take for granted.

While this verse most certainly has a literal sense, it is also metaphorical, for light is often used to refer to the good in life. This becomes clear when we continue to read and see that Qoheleth next encourages his readers to enjoy all the years of their lives, for the "days of darkness will be many." Qoheleth uses "days of darkness" to refer to the difficult times that all people face in life. For people who have lived in a place where the winter is dark, bitter, and seemingly unrelenting, this is a powerful metaphor. Just as the sunlight brings joy to a person, the long nights of a northern winter can begin to wear a person down. All of that darkness is not good for the soul. This memory of darkness—both metaphorical and literal—should cause us to grasp whatever joy is possible whenever God allows it, for we know that the darkness will come again. This advice sounds quite pessimistic, but it is also realistic. Qoheleth looks at life in this world for what it is, thus leading him to offer a way for his readers to cope with the inevitable: rejoice when it is possible, be aware that dark days will come, and remember that they are *hebel*, or fleeting. The transient nature of both the good and the bad in life is encouraging, for people can rest assured that the darkness will not last forever, and it also serves as an impetus to enjoy God's gifts whenever possible.[1]

Qoheleth next encourages his readers to "walk in the ways of your heart and the sight of your eyes," but to remember God's judgment. We will deal with God's judgment extensively in the next lesson, so we will not address it here. Finally, he encourages readers to, as much as they can, remove pain and vexation, both physically and mentally/emotionally. This is an important concept for Qoheleth, who encourages us to take joy in the things that we can enjoy. Part of that entails making the conscious decision to put away pain and vexation while we can. Now, he is not saying that we should feel nothing, refuse to grieve, or self-medicate in

1 Cf., Fredericks, *Ecclesiastes*, 236.

an effort to reduce pain. Rather, this is practical advice intended to encourage his audience not to prolong mental and physical anguish any longer than necessary.

Conclusion: Enjoyment in the Christian Life Today

We have spent this entire lesson looking at Qoheleth's advice for living in a world turned upside-down. We found that, in the end, he encourages us to take joy in the fleeting gifts of God—food, drink, work, and our spouse. That these things are so fleeting provides ever more incentive to take hold of them while we can. We do not know what tomorrow brings, be it death, pain, or joy. Therefore, we must make every effort to take hold of the gifts that God has given. Qoheleth has offered practical advice that each of us can apply to our lives on a regular basis. We should find joy in our work, for it is God's gift to us. Rather than complaining about the tasks he has given us, we should take joy in the ability to do it. It is good to be tired at the end of the day. Likewise, we should take joy in our food, for it is God's gift. It is also crucial to remember to take joy in our spouse, for this is the person whom God has given for us to cherish our entire life. However, we are also reminded that in our quest for enjoyment we must not forget that it is God alone who allows enjoyment. Whatever we take joy in, it comes from the hand of the sovereign God. In our final lesson we will explore the implications of God's sovereignty, our relationship to him, and the importance of obedience.

Discussion Questions

1. This week we examined the *carpe diem* passages in Ecclesiastes in order to understand the other side of Qoheleth's message, which is to rejoice in the face of all of life's injustices, including death. What has God given you that should rejoice in?

2. Thinking through the four areas that we should enjoy—food, drink, work, and one's spouse—how

has God blessed you with these four things? Have you neglected to enjoy these things? If so, what practical steps can you take to be sure that you enjoy them now?

3. After working through this lesson, in what ways can you use the book of Ecclesiastes to minister to a person who is struggling through one of life's injustices that we discussed in the previous lesson?

4. How does the enjoyment aspect of Ecclesiastes intersect with New Testament teaching? Does the New Testament change how we apply the message of Ecclesiastes? Why or why not? If your answer is "yes," then in what way is it changed?

Lesson Six

Objective: Upon completion of this lesson, you will have a clear understanding of the entire message of the book of Ecclesiastes. This lesson seeks to bring together the previous five lessons, as well as explore the role of God's sovereignty and obedience to him in the life of the believer. You will therefore be able to put into context the seemingly divergent voices in Ecclesiastes in a way that makes sense of the book as a whole. Additionally, you will be able to articulate how Ecclesiastes fits into the larger canon of the Bible and is consistent with, and not divergent from, the Bible's overall message and theology. Being able to do this will equip you to minister to those who are hurting, to offer them biblical advice based on Ecclesiastes, and to share with them the message of Ecclesiastes and the Bible as a whole: God is sovereign, loving, and wants to be in relationship with people, which requires our obedience to him.

Opening Prayer: Dear God, thank you for your goodness and grace, and the opportunity to study your Word more deeply. I pray that you will give me the ability to understand the message of Ecclesiastes and to apply it to my life in a way that glorifies you. I pray that you will open my heart and mind to your Word in such a way that it transforms my life and enables me to speak the truth of the gospel to others. Thank you for your sovereignty and the peace that comes with knowing that you are in control and that all good things are from you. Please give me the opportunity to enjoy the gifts that you have given and protect me from the bitterness that so often comes along with unjust suffering. Please also help me not to make gods out of the gifts you've given, and please forgive me for failing to walk obediently in relationship with you. I pray that as I internalize the truth from your Word that you will give me the opportunity to minister to those who also need to hear it.

May your kingdom come and your will be done on earth as it is in heaven. In Jesus's name, Amen

Weekly Reading: Once again, this week we will read the entire book of Ecclesiastes. However, since you've been reading the book consistently for the past five weeks, you have a good understanding of the book's flow and the author's thought process. This week you will only need to read two chapters each day. Since there are only twelve chapters, this leaves you an extra day in case you have to miss a reading. You will also be reading several individual passages in the book as we work through this week's discussion of Ecclesiastes's view of the importance of obedience to God and the overall theology of the book.

Lesson Outline:

1. The importance of obedience to God
2. The overall message of Ecclesiastes

Introduction

We have spent the last five lessons working through various issues in Ecclesiastes with the hopes of arriving at the meaning of the book as a whole. We looked at the identity of Qoheleth, the meaning of the term *hebel*, the book's relationship to the Cain and Abel narrative in Genesis, the book's view of death and injustice, and finally the importance that Ecclesiastes places on taking real joy in God's gifts. We turn now to the importance the book places on obedience to God. We will conclude this lesson, and our study as a whole, with a discussion of the overall message of Ecclesiastes in light of these various factors that influence how we read that book. It is my hope that the study has been beneficial to your life and ministry, and that you will now read Ecclesiastes with fresh eyes and see its beauty and applicability to the church today.

After having spent lessons three and four looking at how Ecclesiastes views death and injustice, we were in danger of viewing the book as an overly pessimistic treatise that rails against God. Indeed, with all the frustration evident in the book, it is no wonder why many scholars have deemed the book the work of a pessimistic sage railing against the machine. Then, in lesson five we looked carefully at many other passages in which Qoheleth balanced his frustration with life with sage advice regarding how to live life in light of the inevitability of death and the presence of injustice. These verses, taken alone, can have the unintended consequence of causing us to believe that the book not only verges on blasphemy against God, but also teaches unfettered hedonism—the quest for pleasure above all things. And so we round out our journey of Ecclesiastes with a discussion of one of the book's primary messages: we humans are accountable to God. There are difficult times we all will face, not the least of which is death itself. In the face of all the suffering to be endured, God has blessed us with temporary gifts that we should grasp tightly. However, we should be careful to enjoy those gifts within the parameters that he has established.

The Importance of Obedience to God

Ecclesiastes 12:13–14

> The end of the matter; all has been heard. Fear God and keep his commandments, for this is the whole duty of man. For God will bring every deed into judgment, with every secret thing, whether good or evil.

We begin our discussion of obedience to God with the final two verses of Ecclesiastes because it is here that we find the hermeneutical lens (i.e. strategy of interpretation) through which to read everything that has come before. While some scholars argue that this verse is a later addition by a pious scribe,[1] we hold to the

1 See, e.g. E.g. K. Siegfried, *Prediger und Hoheslied übersetzt und erklärt* (HAT II, 3/2; Göttingen: Vandenhoeck and Ruprecht, 1898); George A. Barton, *A Critical and Exegetical Commentary on the Book of Ecclesiastes* (ICC; New York: Charles Scribner's Sons), 1908; Kurt Galling, "Kohelet-studien," *ZAW* 50 (1932): 276–99; Martin Rose, *Rien de nouveau:*

book's literary unity.[1] We hold to this position for a few reasons: first, we believe that the Bible should be read as the church reads it, not as the scholars who try to break it apart into what they believe are its constituent parts. As people who approach the Bible from a confessional standpoint, we believe that God superintended the writing of the entire Bible and that the Bible we now have is the one that he intended for us to have. Second, we presuppose that the Bible is a complete unity with a single message, namely that people have rebelled against God and God seeks reconciliation with people, even to the point of sending his own son to die a humiliating death on the cross (Rom 8:32, Phil 2:8). Third, Ecclesiastes is best read as a unity. If we try to pick apart the book, ascribing this verse to one author and that verse to another, then we end up with a tangled mess of conflicting messages. However, if we read the book as a whole and try to understand what appear to be contradictory passages in light of the entire book, then what emerges is a message consistent with itself and with the Bible as a whole. We find that the book is about dealing with life's injustices by enjoying God's gifts and being obedient to him, a message that is not so different from the rest of Scripture, even if it comes to us differently in Ecclesiastes.

In these final two verses of the book we encounter someone speaking in the third person. Most scholars today hold that this voice is that of the "frame narrator," or the person who tells the story of Qoheleth. Throughout most of the book this person relays Qoheleth's words in the first person, but here he reflects on the words of Qoheleth, much as he did in the first part of the book (Eccl 1:1). This does not necessarily mean that the frame narrator is a person different from the book's author, for we have several places

---

Nouvelles approches du livre de Qohélet (Fribourg: Editions Universitaires, 1999).

1 On Ecclesiastes as a literary unity, see esp. Michael V. Fox, "Frame-Narrative and Composition in the Book of Qoheleth," *Hebrew Union College Annual* 48 (1977): 83–106; idem, *Qoheleth and His Contradictions* (JSOT Supplement Series 71; Sheffield: Sheffield Academic, 1989).

throughout the Bible where the author relays his own direct speech, such as in the Pentateuch (Genesis–Deuteronomy). At this point, the author speaks in the third person in order to make certain that his readers have not misunderstood the book as a whole. He does this by stating clearly, "Besides being wise, the Preacher also taught the people knowledge, weighing and studying and arranging many proverbs with great care. The Preacher sought to find words of delight, and uprightly he wrote words of truth" (12:9–10). Thus, the book ends with a statement as to how it should be interpreted—not as the words of a pessimist, but as the words of a realist who honestly reflects on life as it is, but also holds steadfastly to the importance of obedience to and faith in God.

What does the author mean when he states that to "fear God and keep is commandments" is "the whole duty of man"? The term "duty" is not present in the Hebrew, so the phrase could be translated as, "this is the whole of humanity." Perhaps this gives a better sense of what the author is driving at. Is it the duty of humans to fear God and keep his commands? Most certainly, but it goes beyond that. It is not simply the *duty* of humanity to fear and obey God, but it is the *whole* of humanity. That is, relationship with God is at the same time everything and the only thing in life. It is the "whole" of humanity. This certainly includes our duty to walk in right relationship with him, but it includes so much more as well.

This verse also speaks to the important nature of what it means to "fear" God. Fear in the wisdom literature of the Old Testament—and the Bible as a whole—refers to something different than what we usually mean when we speak about fear in our modern context. In the Bible, to fear God is to obey him, to love him, and to walk in right relationship with him. This fear contains some aspect of emotional, fearful response, such as when we have committed sin against him. But, it is much more than that. It is a realization of our proper standing before God and our utter dependence upon him.

As a young boy my grandmother would often sing "Amazing Grace." In the last stages of her battle with cancer I was riding in the car with her, listening to her sing, "'Twas grace that taught my heart to fear, and grace my fears relieved . . ." I thought over that for many years to come. How can I both fear and not fear? After Christ saved me some years later—and still today—I think back on that moment in the car with my dying grandmother and I marvel at the truth of what she was singing. God's grace had taught her to fear God, that is, to live in right relationship with him. And yet, God's grace had also taught her that there is nothing else in life to fear. She would soon be with her Father, and all her pain would dissipate. Maybe she knew I was listening, and maybe not, but that day my grandmother taught me an important lesson about what it means to fear God.

Ecclesiastes ends with the statement that "God will bring every deed into judgment, with every secret thing, whether good or evil." This final statement serves to temper the rest of the book. Should we take great joy in all the things God has given? Yes. Should we eat and drink with great enjoyment? Yes. Should we enjoy the company of a man or woman? Yes. Should we put away vexation and pain? Yes. Should we exhibit a posture of joy and pleasure in life? Yes. But, in doing those things we must remember that God will bring everything we do into judgment. This reminder forms the fence around our enjoyment. We eat and drink, but we must not become gluttons and drunkards. We enjoy the company of a man or woman, but we must do this within the boundaries of marriage between one man and one woman. We take great joy in our work, but we must not become workaholics. We take great pleasure in all of life, but we must not become hedonistic pleasure-seekers. Once we step outside of the God-given boundaries, we enter into sin for which we will be judged.

Ecclesiastes 3:14

> I perceived that whatever God does endures forever; nothing can be added to it, nor anything taken from it. God has done it, so that people fear before him.

This passage is the first time Qoheleth brings up the issue of fearing God. If you think back to our discussion of enjoyment in Ecclesiastes, you will remember that this statement comes just after Qoheleth discusses the importance of knowing the appropriate times for various activities. He concludes by acknowledging God's sovereignty and stating that God has done all he has done for the explicit purpose that people will fear him. James Crenshaw argues that the fear expressed in this passage is markedly different from the fear of God found in Proverbs, which is "the correct attitude of a religious person."[1] In Crenshaw's estimation, fear in Ecclesiastes is terror induced by "an unpredictable despot . . . jealously guarding divine prerogatives."[2] Tremper Longman agrees with Crenshaw's view, stating that "Qoheleth believes that God acts the way that he does to frighten people into submission, not to arouse a sense of respectful awe of his power and might."[3] However, as we noted previously, this section of Ecclesiastes outlines the proper times for activities in life (3:1–8), followed by a discussion of work (3:9–10), God's sovereignty (3:11), and the appropriate human response in the face of uncontrollable circumstances (3:12–13). Nothing in this context demands that we read Qoheleth's statement about fearing God in a negative light.

Therefore, the discussion of fear in Ecclesiastes brings to light the importance of one's presuppositions when reading the book. For, if we read the book pessimistically, then surely we will agree that the fear of God in this context is negative. However, if we think on our discussion of the meaning of *hebel* in Ecclesiastes, we will remember that such a pessimistic reading is unnecessary, even unhelpful. Instead, when we read this passage in the context of the whole book, we find that Qoheleth values fearing God—and that God has caused us to fear him—because it allows for humans to be in relationship with the Lord. Without an appropriate stance before him, and without appropriate obedience to him, there is no hope

---

1 Crenshaw, *Ecclesiastes*, 100.

2 Ibid.

3 Longman, *Ecclesiastes*, 124–25.

for a relationship with him. Yet, God has created the world in such a way as to cause us to fear him, thus opening up the opportunity for us to have a relationship with him.

Ecclesiastes 5:1–7

> Guard your steps when you go to the house of God. To draw near to listen is better than to offer the sacrifice of fools, for they do not know that they are doing evil. Be not rash with your mouth, nor let your heart be hasty to utter a word before God, for God is in heaven and you are on earth. Therefore let your words be few. For a dream comes with much business, and a fool's voice with many words. When you vow a vow to God, do not delay paying it, for he has no pleasure in fools. Pay what you vow. It is better that you should not vow than that you should vow and not pay. Let not your mouth lead you into sin, and do not say before the messenger that it was a mistake. Why should God be angry at your voice and destroy the work of your hands? For when dreams increase and words grow many, there is *hebel*; but God is the one you must fear.

Here Qoheleth returns to the theme of fearing God through a discussion of the appropriate way to act in his house. It is easy in our context to equate the "house of God" with the church building we inhabit on Sunday mornings, but in this context it refers explicitly to the temple. What Qoheleth describes here is common to the biblical ideal of how one should act in God's presence, as Craig Bartholomew points out when he demonstrates the striking parallels between this passage and passages in the book of Proverbs as well as Psalm 40.[1] For example, "In Prov. 1:15–16 and 4:27 feet are used as a graphic symbol for human conduct. Proverbs 1:15–16 exhorts readers to keep 'your foot from their [sinners'] paths, for their feet run to do evil.'"[2] Thus, Qoheleth urges circumspection in the temple, which is entirely in line with the rest of the Old

1 Bartholomew, *Ecclesiastes*, 203–5.

2 Ibid., 203.

Testament teaching about how to approach God. While we no longer enter the temple to offer sacrifices, we should nevertheless remember that God is now present with his people always through the indwelling of the Holy Spirit. This should cause us to walk carefully, knowing that we are always in his presence.

Regarding the "sacrifice of fools," Bartholomew perceptively notes that "The sacrifice of the fools should be thought of not as a denial of the value of sacrifice per se but as a critique of superficial religion that goes through the rituals with many words but no awareness of God."[1] This sentiment is still as powerful and applicable today as it was then. We must be careful to remember that God requires genuine obedience that stems from a relationship with him and a desire to please him. God is not satisfied if we simply go through the motions of godly living but have hearts that are far from him. Jesus develops this same issue quite forcefully in his interactions with the Pharisees. For example, in Matthew 23:23 Jesus states, "Woe to you, scribes and Pharisees, hypocrites! For you tithe the mint and dill and cumin, and have neglected the weightier matters of the law: justice and mercy and faithfulness. These you ought to have done, without neglecting the other." In this passage Jesus is not condemning tithing down to the smallest amount; rather, he is condemning the neglect of the more important matters of the law.[2] In the same way, Qoheleth does not condemn adherence to the law; rather, he condemns the type of law-keeping that ignores what is important—proper relationship with God.

In sum, this passage highlights the importance of fearing God by coupling it with the importance of offering proper sacrifices and remaining silent when appropriate and speaking when appropriate. His statements remind us that we are but small people in the presence of an enormous God. The fear he recommends certainly includes the proper fear that comes from standing in the presence of an awesome God, and yet it also includes the aspects of fear that

---

1 Ibid., 203–204.

2 Thanks to Andrew Higginbotham for pointing this out to me in private conversation.

we find in the rest of the Bible: obedience that develops from a desire to please God and live in right relationship with him. There is nothing in this passage to suggest that Qoheleth views God—or the fear of God—negatively. Rather, he speaks as a person who is well-versed in the theology of Torah (the Pentateuch, or first five books of the Old Testament). His view of fearing God aligns perfectly with the teaching that the proper relationship with God is obedience to and dependence on him.

Ecclesiastes 8:10–13

> Then I saw the wicked buried. They used to go in and out of the holy place and were praised in the city where they had done such things. This also is hebel. Because the sentence against an evil deed is not executed speedily, the heart of the children of man is fully set to do evil. Though a sinner does evil a hundred times and prolongs his life, yet I know that it will be well with those who fear God, because they fear before him. But it will not be well with the wicked, neither will he prolong his days like a shadow, because he does not fear before God.

We have already looked closely at this passage because of its discussion of injustice—the wicked receive a proper burial, access to the holy place, prolonged life, and the praise of others. We also noted that the fact that their sins go unpunished adds insult to injury. For Qoheleth, and for us also, it appears that the wicked prosper while the righteous perish. But in response to this sentiment Qoheleth states in no uncertain terms that it will be better for the righteous "because they fear before him." In the end, the wicked will not prosper, but will suffer their deserved fate. The righteous, on the other hand, will be rewarded for their steadfast obedience to and relationship with God.

As with the previous statements regarding fearing God, this verse appears to some to be out of place, an uncomfortable contradiction to what Qoheleth has said in so many other places. In fact, he appears to contradict himself in only a matter of sentences! Do the wicked prosper or suffer? The answer is yes. Qoheleth speaks in verse 11 of "delayed judgment" that is likely both "human and divine judgment, especially since in Proverbs divine judgment works [among other things] through human agents (cf. Prov. 8:15–16)."[1] In verses 12–13 there is a clear shift from delayed judgment to certain judgment. Qoheleth states that he *knows* that those who do not fear God will suffer judgment at the hands of God, a theme that he visits throughout the book and emphasizes in the final verses of Ecclesiastes. Just as it is with life in the modern world, Qoheleth holds in tension what he believes with what he sees.[2] This is a lesson that we would do well to remember, just like the Psalmist who said,

> But as for me, my feet had almost stumbled, my steps had nearly slipped.
>
> For I was envious of the arrogant when I saw the prosperity of the wicked.
>
> . . .
>
> For behold, those who are far from you shall perish; you put an end to everyone who is unfaithful to you.
>
> But for me it is good to be near God; I have made the Lord God my refuge, that I may tell of all your works. (Ps 73:2–3, 27–28)

Like Qoheleth and the author of Psalm 73, we must remember that God is a just God who will in the end reward faithful obedience to him. So, while it may appear that the wicked prosper while the righteous suffer, we must hold fast to the conviction that fearing God is better than any earthly thing. The judgment of the wicked and prosperity of the righteous may not come in this life, but we can trust that the cross of Christ made it possible for us to live in eternity with God. And even on earth it is better to walk humbly with God than arrogantly with the wicked.

---

1 Bartholomew, *Ecclesiastes*, 290.

2 Ibid., 291.

The Overall Message of Ecclesiastes

This discussion of the importance of fearing God brings us to the end of our lesson and the end of our time together. It remains now only to look back over our discussion to determine what the overall message of Ecclesiastes is and how we can apply it to our lives today. What, then, did Ecclesiastes mean for its original audience, and what does it mean for us today?

Based on our study of the meaning of the term *hebel*, we can affirm that the book is not a pessimistic treatise that reacts strongly to the theology of the rest of the Old Testament. Rather, Qoheleth uses *hebel* to refer to the Cain and Abel narrative to discuss the inconsistencies and injustices he sees in life, the greatest of which is death. Qoheleth looks at the world with *realistic* eyes, not pessimistic ones, and attempts to reconcile what he knows about God with what he sees in the world. Qoheleth uses *hebel* to label various situations that he sees in life because they reflect the same type of inconsistency that occurred when the first human murder occurred. The righteous Abel, who should have lived a long, full life was instead murdered. He was the first righteous person to suffer the fate of the wicked and Cain was the first wicked person to suffer the fate of the righteous, something with which we are all too familiar today. But, Qoheleth does not leave us simply licking our wounds as we complain about life's injustices. He tells us how to live in light of these injustices.

The *carpe diem*, or "seize the day" passages form the other side of the coin for Ecclesiastes. Since there is injustice and wickedness in the world, what are followers of God to do? How should we respond? Qoheleth tells us that we should respond by taking hold of the pleasurable gifts that God has given. If God allows us to enjoy food, companionship, and work, then we should do all we can to enjoy them. The impetus to enjoy is highlighted by the fact that these things are, by their very nature, fleeting. Therefore, we must make every effort to enjoy them *now*.

However, while we are enjoying God's gifts, we must take care to remember that God is the sovereign judge of all the world. In his Word he has given us guidelines for how, when, and to what extent we are to enjoy. We should enjoy food, but we must not be gluttons. We should enjoy an intimate relationship with another human being, but only our spouse. While we are taking hold of the gifts God has given, we must be ever mindful of the fact that he will judge sin. We must therefore remain obedient to him throughout our lives so that we might live in right relationship with him.

Bringing these three aspects of the message of Ecclesiastes together, we can say that the overall message of Ecclesiastes is how to live life in relationship with God when it appears to the human eye that he is nowhere to be found. Ecclesiastes teaches us to do this through honest reflection on life as we see it, enjoyment of God's gifts, and fear of God that results in and is manifested through obedience to him.

Discussion Questions

1. How does the message of Ecclesiastes fit with the message of the rest of the Bible? Are there areas of apparent contradiction? How are these resolved?

2. Having studied Ecclesiastes in detail, what are some of the most important take-away points from your study? What aspects of the book were made clearer by your study? Is there anything in the book that you would like to study in more detail?

3. How does the idea that we should enjoy God's gifts within his boundaries confront the culture of pleasure in which we live today? Are you surprised that a book of the Bible encourages enjoyment in the human pleasures of life?

4. What does it mean to live in fear of and obedience to God? What is your understanding of the fear of God? Is it similar to

that of Ecclesiastes? If not, how can you change your thinking so that it lines up with what Scripture teaches?

Bibliography

Bartholomew, Craig G. *Ecclesiastes*. Baker Commentary on the Old Testament Wisdom and Psalms. Grand Rapids, MI: Baker Academic, 2009.

_____. "The Theology of Ecclesiastes." Pages 367–86 in *The Words of the Wise are Like Goads: Engaging Qoheleth in the 21st Century*. Edited by Mark J. Boda, Tremper Longman III, and Cristian Rata. Winona Lake, IN: Eisenbrauns, 2013.

Bartholomew, Craig G. and Ryan O'Dowd. *Old Testament Wisdom Literature: A Theological Introduction*. Downers Grove, IL: InterVarsity, 2011.

Barton, George A. *A Critical and Exegetical Commentary on the Book of Ecclesiastes*. ICC. New York: Charles Scribner's Sons, 1908.

Bollhagen, James. *Ecclesiastes*. Concordia Commentary. St. Louis, MO: Concordia, 2011.

Brown, Stephen G. "The Structure of Ecclesiastes." *Evangelical Review of Theology* 14 (1990): 195–208.

Brown, William P. *Ecclesiastes*. Interpretation. Louisville, KY: John Knox, 2000.

Brueggemann, Walter. "Bounded by Obedience and Praise: The Psalms as Canon," *Journal for the Study of the Old Testament* 50 (1991): 63–92.

Beldman, David J. H. "Framed! Structure in Ecclesiastes." Pages 137–61 in *The Words of the Wise are Like Goads: Engaging Qoheleth in the 21st Century*. Edited by Mark J. Boda, Tremper Longman III, and Cristian Rata. Winona Lake, IN: Eisenbrauns, 2013.

Bonaventure. *St. Bonaventure's Commentary on Ecclesiastes*. Edited and translated by R. J. Karris and C. Murray. Bonaventure, NY: Franciscan, 2005.

Bonhoeffer, Dietrich. *Letters and Papers from Prison*. Translated by Reginald H. Fuller and Frank Clarke. Edited by Eberhard Bethge. New York: Macmillan, 1972.

Brenner, A. *Colour Terms in the Old Testament*. JSOT Supplement 21. Sheffield: JSOT Press, 1982.

Christianson, Eric S. *A Time To Tell: Narrative Strategy in Ecclesiastes*. JSOT Supplement 280. Sheffield: Sheffield Academic, 1998.

_____. *Ecclesiastes through the Centuries*. Blackwell Bible Commentaries. Malden, MA: Blackwell, 2007.

Cohen, A., translator. *Midrash Rabbah Ecclesiastes*. 3rd ed. Volume 8. New York: Soncino, 1983.

Coppins, Joseph. "La structure de l'Ecclesiate." Pages 288–92 in *La Sagesse de l'Ancien Testament*. Edited by Maurice Gilbert. Paris: Gembloux, 1979.

Crenshaw, James. *Ecclesiastes*. Old Testament Library. Louisville, KY: Westminster, 1987.

Duvall, J. Scott and J. Daniel Hays, *Grasping God's Word: A Hands-On Approach to Reading, Interpreting, and Applying the Bible*. 3rd ed. Grand Rapids, MI: Zondervan, 2012.

Estes, Daniel J. *Handbook on the Wisdom Books and Psalms: Job, Psalms, Proverbs, Ecclesiastes, Song of Songs*. Grand Rapids, MI: Baker Academic, 2005.

Farmer, K. *Who Knows What is Good? A Commentary on the Books of Proverbs and Ecclesiastes*. International Theological Commentary. Grand Rapids, MI: Eerdmans, 1991.

Fishbane, Michael. *Biblical Interpretation in Ancient Israel*. Oxford: Oxford University Press, 1985.

Fox, Michael V. "Frame-Narrative and Composition in the Book of Qoheleth." *Hebrew Union College Annual* 48 (1977): 83–106.

_____. "The Meaning of *Hebel* for Qoheleth." *Journal of Biblical Literature* 105 (1986): 409–27.

_____. *Qoheleth and His Contradictions.* JSOT Supplement 71. Sheffield: Sheffield Academic, 1989.

_____. "The Inner Structure of Qoheleth's Thought." Pages 225–38 in *Qoheleth in the Context of Wisdom.* Edited by Antoon Schoors. Leeuven: Leeuven University Press, 1998.

_____. *A Time to Tear Down and a Time to Build Up: A Rereading of Ecclesiastes.* Grand Rapids, MI: Eerdmans, 1999.

Fredericks, Daniel. *Qoheleth's Language: Re-Evaluating Its Nature and Date.* Ancient Near Eastern Texts and Studies 3. Lewiston, NY: Edwin Mellen, 1989.

_____. *Coping with Transience: Ecclesiastes on the Brevity in Life.* The Biblical Seminar 18. Sheffield: JSOT, 1993.

Fredericks, Daniel and Daniel J. Estes. *Ecclesiastes and Song of Songs.* Apollos Old Testament Commentary. Downers Grove, IL: InterVarsity, 2010.

Galling, Kurt. Kohelet-studien." *Zeitschrift für die alttestamentliche Wissenschaft* 50 (1932): 276–99.

Gammie, John G. "Theology of Retribution in the Book of Deuteronomy." *Catholic Biblical Quarterly* 32 (1970): 1–12.

Garrett, Duane. *Proverbs, Ecclesiastes, Song of Songs.* New American Commentary 14. Nashville, TN: Broadman, 1993.

Gordis, Robert. *Koheleth—The Man and His World.* 3rd edition. New York: Shocken, 1968.

Greidanus, Sidney. *Preaching Christ from Ecclesiastes: Foundations for Expository Sermons.* Grand Rapids, MI: Eerdmans, 2012.

Gunkel, Hermann. *Genesis.* Translated by Mark E. Biddle. Mercer Library of Biblical Studies. Macon, GA: Mercer University Press, 1997.

Jellicoe, Sidney. *The Septuagint and Modern Study.* Ann Arbor, MI: Eisenbrauns, 1978.

Kaiser, Walter C, Jr. *Toward an Old Testament Theology*. Grand Rapids, MI: Zondervan, 1978.

_____. *Ecclesiastes: Total Life*. Everyman's Bible Commentary. Chicago: Moody, 1979.

_____. *The Promise-Plan of God: A Biblical Theology of the Old and New Testaments*. Grand Rapids, MI: Zondervan, 2008.

Kitchen, Kenneth. *The Bible in Its World: The Bible and Archaeology Today*. Eugene, OR: Wipf and Stock, 2004.

Knobel, Peter S., editor. *The Targum of Qoheleth*. The Aramaic Bible 15. Edinburgh: T & T Clark, 1991.

Lavoie, J. J. "*Habel habalim hakol habel*: Historie de l'interprétation d'une formule celebre et enjeux culturels." *Science et Esprit* 53 (2006): 219–49.

Van Leeuwen. "Wealth and Poverty: System and Contradiction in Proverbs." *Hebrew Studies* 33 (1992): 25–36.

Limburg, James. *Encountering Ecclesiastes: A Book for Our Time*. Grand Rapids, MI: Eerdmans, 2006.

Longman, Tremper, III. *The Book of Ecclesiastes*. New International Commentary on the Old Testament. Grand Rapids, MI: Eerdmans, 1998.

Luther, Martin. *An Exposition of Salomons Booke Called Ecclesiastes or the Preacher*. London: John Daye, 1573.

_____. *Luther's Works*. Saint Louis: Concordia, 1972.

Meek, Russell. "The Meaning of הבל in Ecclesiastes: An Intertextual Suggestion." Pages 241–56 in *The Words of the Wise are Like Goads: Engaging Qoheleth in the 21st Century*. Edited by Mark J. Boda, Tremper Longman III, and Cristian Rata. Winona Lake, IN: Eisenbrauns, 2013.

Miller, Douglas. "Power in Wisdom: The Suffering Servant of Ecclesiastes 4." Pages 145–73 in *Peace and Justice Shall Embrace: Power and Theopolitics in the Bible, Essays in Honor of Millard Lind*. Edited by Ted Grimsrud and Loren Johns. Telford, PA: Pandora, 1999.

_____. *Symbol and Rhetoric in Ecclesiastes: The Place of Hebel in Qoheleth's Work*. Academia Biblical 2. Atlanta: Society of Biblical Literature, 2002.

O'Dowd, Ryan. *The Wisdom of Torah: Epistemology in Deuteronomy and the Wisdom Literature*. Forschungen zur Religion und Literatur des Alten und Neuen Testaments 225. Göttingen: Vandenhoeck and Ruprecht, 2009.

Ogden, Graham. *Qoheleth*. Readings: A New Biblical Commentary. 2nd ed. Sheffield: Sheffield Phoenix, 2007.

_____. "Vanity It Certainly is Not." *The Bible Translator* 38: (1987): 301–307.

Osborne, Grant O. *The Hermeneutical Spiral: A Comprehensive Introduction to Biblical Interpretation*. Revised and Expanded ed. Downers Grove, IL: IVP Academic, 2006.

Pinker, Aaron. "The Advantage of a Country in Ecclesiastes 5:8." *Jewish Bible Quarterly* 37 (2009): 211–22.

Preston, Theodore. *The Hebrew Text, and a Latin Version of the Book of Solomon Called Ecclesiastes; with Original Notes, Philological and Exegetical, and a Translation of the Commentary of Mendlessohn from the Rabbinic Hebrew; Also a Newly Arranged Version of Ecclesiastes*. London: John W. Parker, 1845.

Pritchard, J. B., editor. *Ancient Near Eastern Texts Relating to the Old Testament*. 3rd ed. Princeton: Princeton University Press, 1969

von Rad, Gerhard. *A Commentary on Genesis*. Translated by Ford L. Battles. Library of Christian Classics 20. Philadelphia: Westminster, 1972.

Rendtorff, Rolf. *Canon and Theology: Overtures to an Old Testament Theology*. Translated and edited by Margaret Kohl. Overtures to Biblical Theology. Minneapolis: Fortress, 1993.

Rose, Martin. *Rien de nouveau: Nouvelles approches du livre de Qohélet*. Fribourg: Editions Universitaires, 1999.

Routledge, Robin. *Old Testament Theology: A Thematic Approach*. Downers Grove, IL: IVP Academic, 2008.

Sailhammer, J. *The Meaning of the Pentateuch: Revelation, Composition, and Interpretation*. Downers Grove, IL: IVP Academic, 2009.

Siegfried, K. *Prediger und Hoheslied übersetzt und erklärt*. Handbuch zum Alten Testament II, 3/2. Göttingen: Vandenhoeck and Ruprecht, 1898.

Sneed, Mark. "Is the 'Wisdom Tradition' a Tradition?" *Catholic Biblical Quarterly* 73 (2011): 50–71.

Seow, C L. *Ecclesiastes: A New Translation with Introduction and Commentary*. Anchor Bible 18C. New York: Doubleday, 1997.

_____."Beyond Mortal Grasp: The Usage of *hebel* in Ecclesiastes." *Australian Biblical Review* 48 (2000): 1–16.

Soulen, Richard N. and R. Kendall Soulen. *Handbook of Biblical Criticism*. 3d ed. Louisville, KY: Westminster John Knox, 2001.

Verheijj, Arian. "Paradise Retried: On Qoheleth 2:4–6." *Journal for the Study of the Old Testament* 50 (1991): 113–115.

Waltke, Bruce with Charles Yu. *An Old Testament Theology: An Exegetical, Canonical, and Thematic Approach*. Grand Rapids, MI: Zondervan, 2007.

Weinfeld, Moshe. *Deuteronomy and the Deuteronomic School.* Oxford: Clarendon, 1972.

Westermann, Claus. *Genesis 1–11*. Continental Commentary. Translated by John J. Scullion. Minneapolis, MN: Fortress, 1997.

Wright, Addison G. "Riddle of the Sphinx: The Structure of the Book of Qoheleth." *Catholic Biblical Quarterly* 30 (1968): 313–34.

Wright, Robert J., editor. *Proverbs, Ecclesiastes, and Song of Solomon*. Ancient Christian Commentary on Scripture IX. Downers Grove, IL: InterVarsity, 2005.

Würthwein, Ernst. *The Text of the Old Testament: An Introduction to the Biblica Hebraica.* 2nd Revised and Enlarged ed. Translated by Erroll F. Rhodes. Grand Rapids, MI: Eerdmans, 1998.

Appendix A:

Participatory Study Method

How can I get more from my Bible reading?

There is no shortcut in Bible study. If you want to find what God has for you in Scripture you will have to dig. There are some things you can do to make your study time more profitable. In this appendix you will find an outline to an approach to Bible study that can help you both with devotional reading and with deeper study.

PREPARATION

Gather Materials – have pen, paper, highlighters or other markers and all materials you will need for study available.

Conditions – Find a place where you can study. If you study well with music playing, put some on. If you prefer quiet, arrange for a quiet place.

Resources – Get a small, well-selected set of study materials. For suggestions see the resource list in appendix B.

Prayer – As you begin your study, consider the premise that Scripture comes to us as God-breathed, and therefore it is "useful for teaching for reproof, for correction, and for training in righteousness, so that everyone who belongs to God may be proficient, equipped for every good work" (2 Timothy 3:16- 17 NRSV). Keeping in mind this word, share in this prayer:

Eternal God, in the reading of the Scripture, may your word be heard; in the meditations of our hearts, may your word be known;

and in the faithfulness of our lives, may your word be shown. Amen.

(*Chalice Worship,* 384).

GET AN OVERVIEW OF THE PASSAGE

Read the passage multiple times. Any number from three times up will help. Memorizing is useful, at least of key texts. (This will also require you to select key texts.) Read from different Bible versions, to help you with your concentration, and to open up different ways of understanding the passage. At this point don't use commentaries, study notes, your concordance, or anything which takes your concentration off of the passage you are studying.

STUDY THE BACKGROUND

Find out who wrote the passage, to whom it was written, what is the situation being addressed, and what type of literature it is.

MEDITATE, QUESTION, RESEARCH, COMPARE (REPEAT AS NEEDED)

Meditate on the passage. If you are having difficulty meditating, think about telling someone else about the passage, such as a friend in need of encouragement, someone who is struggling with their faith or asking questions about faith, or a child. Think: What questions might they ask about this passage? You can formulate thought questions or fact questions. Fact questions focus on what the author is actually saying. Thought questions may lead you to other revelations that lay well beyond the intended statement of the passage.

You might consider creating an outline of the passage, compare it with other Scriptures or with the writings of figures in church history, or even to current experience.

Ask: What similar experience are we having today? Could this help me better understand the passage. For example, if you have had a vision, might this help you understand the vision recorded in Ezekiel 1? Ask your friends about experiences they have had. You might consult historical figures such as: Jerome, Aquinas, Teresa of Avila, Augustine, Martin Luther, John Wesley, John Calvin, Karl Barth, and many others.

SHARE YOUR THOUGHTS

Ask yourself how this text has been applied in your experience. Get to know the person you are sharing with. Share your experience and then the text. Always work from your own personal experience with God. Store up the experiences your friends share with you to use in studying further Scripture.

The purpose of sharing is not just to help others with your own insight. It is also intended to provide a check on what you think you have learned. It is easy to get off track in independent Bible study. Sharing helps keep you a part of the community. Make sure that some of your sharing is with people who have experience and training in study. Training and degrees do not guarantee accuracy, but it does provide a valuable check.

EXAMPLE PASSAGE 1 KINGS 19:11-18

1. Begin your study with prayer.
2. Read the passage several times. Can you tell this story in your own words?
    - e) Read 1 Kings 17-19. Check a Bible dictionary or study Bible for the background of 1Kings.
    - f) Consider how Elijah feels through this experience.
    - g) Consider what God is trying to accomplish by giving Elijah these experiences.
    - h) How did Elijah know the Lord was not in the wind, the earthquake or the fire?
    - i) Can the Lord appear in such violent events? (Use your concordance, looking up wind, fire, and earthquake.)

j) Does God respond to Elijah's complaint? (Only indirectly; he gives him a task.)
k) Is Elijah as much alone as he feels he is? (No, there are 7,000 more faithful people, v. 18.)
l) What other Bible characters have experienced something similar to this? (Daniel 3—the fiery furnace.)
m) What people in church history may have experienced something similar to this? (Any martyr or person who has suffered persecution.)
n) Have you experienced similar feelings? Have you ever felt completely alone in your faith?

3. Share your experiences!!

EXAMPLE PRAYER FOR BIBLE STUDY

Lord, take from me any thought habits which will keep me from hearing. Make me open to your voice and your voice alone. Lord, help me to accept your people as my brothers and sisters in your kingdom and let me learn and grow from both their weaknesses and their strengths. Lord, I trust you to reveal yourself to your people the way you know is best. Let your will be done. Lord, let me not only recognize but obey your voice. Let my actions be conformed to your will. Help me to love my neighbor as myself. In Jesus' name, Amen.

Appendix B:

Tools for Bible Study

The following are some suggested resources for Bible study. They fall into eight categories:

BIBLE VERSIONS

You will need a Bible version that you can understand without having to consult an English dictionary too often.

✓ For quick reading (overview):

» *Contemporary English Version* (CEV)

3rd or 4th grade reading level; high degree of accuracy within the context of its aim for easy readability.

» *The Cotton Patch Version* by Clarence Jordan

An interpretive paraphrase reflecting rural Georgian dialect and culture.

» *The Message*

Heavily paraphrased with cultural terms translated. This version is fun to read, but will tend to obscure elements of the original cultures.

» *New Living Translation* (NLT)

A more accurate revision of the Living Bible. This is the easy-reading Bible for evangelical Christians.

» *Today's New International Vernon*

Shows its relationship to the popular NIV in many wordings, but uses simplified language and sentence structure in many cases.

✓ For study or reading:

» *Common English Bible* (CEB)

A new translation sponsored by Mainline Protestant publishing houses, the CEB attempts to combine high level scholarship with readability. The New Testament was published in 2010, with the complete Bible available in 2011.

» *New International Version* (NIV)

The NIV is a dynamic equivalent translation of the Bible that is popular among evangelical Christians. A new revision of this translation appeared in electronic form in 2010 and will be available in print in 2011

» New Revised Standard Version (NRSV)

The descendant of the Revised Standard Version, it is the Bible of choice for mainline Christians needing a study Bible. It is known for its attempt to use gender neutral language where appropriate.

» *Revised English Bible* (REB)

This version was translated by an interdenominational committee with interfaith review, that exhibits the different texture of British English.

» *New American Standard Bible* (NASB)

A very formal rendering of the original languages, the NASB has its roots in conservative evangelicalism. It can be wooden and difficult to read.

STUDY BIBLES

Study Bibles usually contain introductory articles giving Bible backgrounds, information on methodology and overviews of various themes in the Bible. They will also include introductions to each book and comments on difficult passages. Study Bibles will reflect religious views of editors and authors, some more than others. Care should be taken to distinguish the Biblical text from the comments, and facts and opinions within the comments.

✓ *New Interpreter} Study Bible* (NRSV)

This new study Bible includes extensive historical and theological annotations, good introductions and outlines, and excursuses giving further background and insight regarding particular themes and passages.

✓ *New Oxford Annotated Bible* (NRSV)

A standard scholarly study Bible, often used in universities and seminaries.

✓ *HarperCollins Study Bible* (NRSV)

Carrying the sponsorship of the Society of Biblical Literature, it has Mainstream or liberal notes with acknowledgment of more conservative options.

✓ *Oxford Study Bible* (REB)

✓ *The NIV Study Bible* (Zondervan)

Popular among evangelicals, bringing a more conservative approach to the Bible.

✓ *ESV Study Bible*

A new Reformed standard study.

✓ *NLT Study Bible*

Based on the popular, easy-to-read New Living Translation, this evangelical study Bible provides extensive notes on both background and application.

BIBLE HANDBOOKS

Bible handbooks provide historical and cultural information, usually with a number of general articles and then comments on particular books and passages. Using a Bible handbook along with your Bible is like having a Bible with study notes, though usually having a handbook in a separate volume will mean that the handbook contains more exhaustive information. Bible handbooks, like study Bibles, will reflect religious presuppositions of the editors. Use them carefully.

- ✓ Mainstream and/or Liberal
  - » *The Cambridge Companion to the Bible O:iford Companion to the Bible*
- ✓ Moderate
  - » *Eerdman's Handbook to the Bible*
- ✓ Conservative
  - » *Zondervan's Handbook to the Bible*

BACKGROUND DOCUMENTS

✓ Pritchard, James. *Ancient Near Eastern Texts*

Large, expensive, hard cover but a tremendous resource for the Bible student.

✓ Pritchard, James. *The Ancient Near East, Volume 1, An Anthology of Texts and Pictures*

(Both 1958 and 1975 editions still available)

✓ Charlesworth, James H. *The Old Testament Pseudepigrapha* (2 volumes).

This work is a standard for editions of these extra-biblical works.

BIBLE COMMENTARIES

Bible commentaries are designed to provide introductions, background, and interpretation of biblical texts. They come in many forms, ranging from one-volume efforts to commentaries on individual books. Many commentaries appear in sets, but with few exceptions, when purchasing commentaries on individual books of the Bible it is better to buy these individually rather than in sets. There are a few exceptions, such as with the New Interpreter's Bible, which is something of a hybrid. It is important to stay away from older, dated commentaries, except perhaps for devotional or theological reasons. In many online programs you will find commentaries such as Matthew Henry's, which is in public domain and thus free to publish without copyright infringement. It is, however, an 18th century product. A good place to start for any library is a solid, up-to-date one-volume commentary.

- ✓ Mainstream
  - » *New Interpreter's Bible*, 12 volumes (Abingdon)

A replacement for the venerable Interpreter's Bible, this is a mainstream commentary set drawing its authors from across the Christian community, including evangelical, mainline, Catholic, and Orthodox scholars.

  - » *New Interpeter's One Volume Commentary* (Abingdon)

Based on the principles of the much larger multi-volume edition, it is a completely new commentary and not simply an abridgement.

  - » *HarperCollins Bible Commentary* (HarperOne)

As with the HarperCollins Bible Dictionary, this commentary is sponsored by the Society of Biblical Literature.

  - » *People's New Testament Commentary of the New Testament* (WJK Press)

This commentary on the New Testament is written by two Disciples of Christ scholars, Fred Craddock and Eugene Boring.

  - » *The New Jerome Bible Commentary*, 3rd edition (Prentice Hall)

This is a predominantly Roman Catholic commentary, authored and edited by highly regarded critical scholars.

- ✓ Evangelical
  - » *Eerdmans Commentary on the Bible*

This work is very compatible with mainstream scholarship, but comes from a publisher that stands as a bridge between evangelical and mainline Protestantism.

  - » *New Bible Commentary: 21st Century edition* (IVP)

BIBLE CONCORDANCES

Concordances may be exhaustive, complete, or concise. Usage of these terms is not 100% consistent. In addition they may either be either organized by words or topics. Many Bibles contain small, concise concordances. Many study Bibles contain topical concordances. Exhaustive concordances contain every reference to a word listed under every word. Complete concordances contain references to each and every verse, using significant terms, though not necessarily under every word in the verse. Concise concordances contain selective references and may not reference all verses. Topical concordances provide a guide to topics covered by specific texts. This can be helpful, but one must always remember that unlike a typical concordance, which is rooted in word usage, this type is more likely to be driven by theological presuppositions.

Concordances with Greek and/or Hebrew Lexicons can be useful, but one should remember that translation is not as simple as just picking a word from a dictionary definition. Context always determines usage and meaning.

- ✓ Exhaustive with Greek/Hebrew
  - » *Strong's Exhaustive Concordance.*

  It is part of the public domain and is regularly reprinted. It is based on the KJV and an older lexicon. It's numbering system and lexicon has served as the model for other concordances

  - » *The NIV Exhaustive Concordance* (Zondervan)

  Based completely on the NIV, it goes beyond Strong's.

  - » *New American Standard Exhaustive Concordance of the Bible/Hebrew-Aramaic and Greek Dictionaries*
  - » *New American Standard Strong's Exhaustive Concordance*

  Based on the Strong's Concordance system, it is keyed to the NASB.

- ✓ Exhaustive Concordances
  - » *NRSV Concordance Unabridged* (Zondervan)
- ✓ Complete Concordances
  - » *Cruden's Complete Concordance Concordance to the KJV.*

  This is an 18th century product, but because it is public domain it is regularly reprinted.

- ✓ Concise Concordances
  - » *The Concise Concordance to the New Revised Standard Version* (Oxford)
- ✓ Topical Concordances
  - » *Holman Concise Topical Concordance* (Holman Reference)
  - » *Topical Analysis of the Bible* (Baker)

BIBLE DICTIONARIES

Bible dictionaries provide definitions of various biblical terms, information about places and people, and introductory information about biblical books. Most information contained in a Bible handbook can be found in a Bible dictionary, but it will be organized much differently.

The religious views of authors and editors will impact the content of a Bible dictionary, as it does with a handbook or commentary. When purchasing a Bible dictionary, it is always best to purchase one that has been authored/ edited by reputable scholars, is even-handed in its approach, and is up-to-date.

- ✓ Mainstream
  - » *HarperCollins Bible Dictionary, Revised Edition.* (HarperOne)
  - » *A Dictionary of the Bible, 2nd ed.* (Oxford University Press)

Based upon the *Harper-Collins Bible Dictionary,* this is a more up-to-date expansion.

- » *Anchor Bible Dictionary*, 6 volumes (Doubleday)
- » *Eerdman's Dictionary of the Bible*
- » *New Interpreter's Dictionary of the Bible,* 5 volumes, (Abingdon)

✓ Evangelical

- » *New International Bible Dictionary* (Zondervan)
- » *New Bible Dictionary*, 3''' edition. (Intervarsity Press)
- » *Zondervan Encyclopedia of the Bible*, Revised Edition (5 volumes)

BIBLE ATLASES

Bible atlases, as one might presume, contain maps and related background materials that assist students of the Bible placing texts and individuals in their proper historical and geographical context. It is important once again to stress the need for up-to-date reference works. It is also important to note that theology once again impacts the results of the work-knowing the background of a publisher can be helpful in this. Therefore, Harper-Collins is probably more mainstream and cross-confessional, while IVP and Zondervan will be more evangelical or conservative.

✓ *HarperCollins Concise Atlas of the Bible.* (HarperOne)

In paperback and at 152 pages, this one may be all the average Bible student needs.

✓ *The MacMillan Bible Atlas*, 3rd edition. (MacMillan)

This has been a standard atlas, which is marked by the editorship of Jewish scholars.

- ✓ *The Biblical World* (National Geographic)
- ✓ *Harper Collins Atlas of Bible History* (HarperOne)
- ✓ *Oxford Bible Atlas* (Oxford University Press)
- ✓ *The IVP Atlas of Bible History* (IVP)
- ✓ Zondervan Atlas of the Bible (Zondervan)

SOME DEFINITIONS

Note: Labels in connection with many of these resources can be misleading. No label is to be regarded as either pejorative or complimentary. "Mainstream" doesn't mean "correct," for example.

Mainstream: Materials which would be suitable for use in departments of religion at secular universities. This does not imply more or less correct in content

Interfaith: Involving persons other than those of one faith (Christians and Jews, for example). Distinguish from interdenominational.

Interdenominational: Involving persons from more than one Christian denomination. Distinguish from interfaith. Only minimal bibliographical information is given in this appendix. It should be enough to locate materials in Books in Print or via online services such as Amazon.com or Barnes and Noble. For further information on resources, check the Participatory Bible Study web page. http:/ /www.deepbiblestudy.com.

More from Energion Publications

Personal Study

Holy Smoke! Unholy Fire	Bob McKibben	$14.99
The Jesus Paradigm	David Alan Black	$17.99
When People Speak for God	Henry Neufeld	$17.99
The Sacred Journey	Chris Surber	$11.99

Christian Living

Faith in the Public Square	Robert D. Cornwall	$16.99
Grief: Finding the Candle of Light	Jody Neufeld	$8.99
Crossing the Street	Robert LaRochelle	$16.99

Bible Study

Learning and Living Scripture	Lentz/Neufeld	$12.99
From Inspiration to Understanding	Edward W. H. Vick	$24.99
Luke: A Participatory Study Guide	Geoffrey Lentz	$8.99
Philippians: A Participatory Study Guide	Bruce Epperly	$9.99
Ephesians: A Participatory Study Guide	Robert D. Cornwall	$9.99

Theology

Creation in Scripture	Herold Weiss	$12.99
Creation: the Christian Doctrine	Edward W. H. Vick	$12.99
The Politics of Witness	Allan R. Bevere	$9.99
Ultimate Allegiance	Robert D. Cornwall	$9.99
History and Christian Faith	Edward W. H. Vick	$9.99
The Church Under the Cross	William Powell Tuck	$11.99
The Journey to the Undiscovered Country	William Powell Tuck	$9.99
Eschatology: A Participatory Study Guide	Edward W. H. Vick	$9.99

Ministry

Clergy Table Talk	Kent Ira Groff	$9.99
Out of This World	Darren McClellan	$24.99
Wind and Whirlwind	David Moffett-Moore	$9.99

www.ingramcontent.com/pod-product-compliance
Lightning Source LLC
LaVergne TN
LVHW092324080426
835508LV00039B/524